❊ Enriching Faith ❊

LESSONS AND ACTIVITIES ON WHAT MAKES US CATHOLIC

JANET SCHAEFFLER, OP

TWENTY THIRD 23rd
PUBLICATIONS
www.23rdpublications.com

TWENTY-THIRD PUBLICATIONS
A Division of Bayard
One Montauk Avenue, Suite 200
New London, CT 06320
(860) 437-3012 or (800) 321-0411
www.23rdpublications.com

ISBN: 978-1-62785-082-7
Library of Congress Control Number: 2015935689
Printed in the U.S.A.

CONTENTS

INTRODUCTION

As Catholics, we have a treasure chest of customs, traditions, rituals, and symbols, all of them reminding us who we are and how we live as disciples. This book explores just a few of them.

I hope the ideas here will lead children and youth to understand these treasures more deeply and to live them more faithfully—all in creative, engaging, enjoyable, and engrossing activities.

Many of these activities can be changed and adapted to explore other symbols, rituals, and customs of our faith. In choosing and working with activities, remember nine noteworthy necessities:

❶ **Activities are theologically sound.** All that we do needs to help learners delve deeper into and remember the meaning. Oftentimes, our choice of activities might concentrate on the details (not that details aren't important) but neglect the core meaning, the religious import.

In studying the creation story, for example, rather than drawing (or coloring) seven pictures of the seven days, making a room-length mural of all of creation, with the words "God saw that it was good," emphasizes the foundational meaning.

Rather than some type of project concentrating upon all the animals in the story of Noah's Ark (cute as it might be), a large rainbow filled with some of God's promises recorded in Scripture would depict the scriptural meaning of the story: God keeps promises.

❷ **Activities are catechetically/ educationally valuable.** Activities are used to deepen the learner's understanding or appreciation of the theme by illuminating the truth, the personal implications of the belief, and the relevance of faith.

Rather than simply reviewing by inviting the children/youth to list/make a poster of the Corporal Works of Mercy, invite various pairs/ groups of learners to draw a picture, or do a PowerPoint or video, of how each work is or can be lived by those their own age.

❸ **Activities belong to the learner.** The essence of the activity is self-expression: how does what we have just learned apply to my life? Therefore, there is no need for patterns or samples to illustrate "what it has to look like." There are no rules proclaiming "it has to be *this* way."

Because the activity helps the learners interpret and deepen—not just repeat—what has been learned, it takes them beyond the presentation. After a study of the Psalms, rewriting a psalm in one's own words or writing a psalm for today, from the learners' everyday experiences/needs, will help to make the meaning of psalms more personal.

After a discussion on God: if you were to paint God, what color would you select?

After the Scripture story of Zacchaeus: if you were Zacchaeus, what would you say in a thank-you note?

❹ **Activities touch upon each person's creativity.** The skilled catechist invites the children/youth, saying just enough to spark their thoughts but leaving them with freedom so that they can imagine, dream, think, and apply.

Rather than doing a puzzle, or a fill in the blanks, etc., about the call of the disciples, children/youth can be invited to imagine they were there; they were called by Jesus. They might write a letter to their family about what happened, their feelings about it, and what they will now do.

Rather than using a word game that only uses memory, create a newspaper about a Scripture event or a billboard that advertises God's love; this approach calls upon individual creativity and imagination and deepens learning and appreciation.

❺ Activities take various expressions. Activities are much more than crossword puzzles, drawing pictures, etc. Wouldn't it be wonderful if each new session invited the learners to respond through a new type of media, different materials, participative experiences, employing the various creative expressions of our heritage, of who we are as humans?

❻ Everyone doesn't need to do the same thing. Children/youth will have different abilities and interests. Whenever possible, suggest options for any given session. Within a lesson on prayer, for example, give four options from which they can choose: using paint, show what you feel when praying alone or with others; rewrite the *Magnificat* in your own words; design gestures to accompany your favorite psalm; select a popular song that can be used as prayer accompanied by PowerPoint.

❼ Activities aren't fillers. In lesson planning, catechists don't dream things up just to keep the learners busy. Activities/projects flow from the theme and reinforce the core teaching.

Neither do activities have to always take place at the end of the session, during the last ten minutes. At the very beginning, invite the learners to mold a sculpture from clay that expresses their idea of God's forgiveness. These sculptures can then be referred to throughout the session and might be a focal point for a closing prayer service.

❽ Activities relate to life outside the group session. Faith formation sessions, of course, are never an end in themselves. They send children/youth forth to a life of discipleship, a life of prayer and witness, a life of serving in their everyday lives. All learning answers the "so what?" question. What does this truth, doctrine, belief, or practice of our heritage have to do with my everyday life?

Invite the learners to interview someone, such as the owner of a store or the principal of a school, about respect for property and possessions. How do these real-life encounters deepen the discussion and learning that happened during the session?

❾ Utilize the full potential of each activity. Even though the process (what happens within) is more important than the finished product, learners quickly figure out what is/what isn't busy work by the way catechists care for and take an interest in their work.

The more useful the better: with pictures of children living the Beatitudes, don't just post them. Compare, discuss, make an album, show and explain to another class; display in the church gathering space; publish.

The more prayerful the better: write a prayer to accompany a drawing or activity; bring written/drawn activities in procession to the prayer corner to use/to offer during prayer.

1 ADVENT

Objective
To prepare for the season of Advent by making Family Envelopes of Activities

Background for Catechists
The liturgical year begins four weeks before Christmas. Advent means "coming"; we celebrate the three comings of Jesus: into our world some two thousand years ago, the Second Coming in the future, and how Jesus comes each day into our lives. Advent calls us to slow down and reflect on the gift of Jesus in our lives. Yet, in many ways, with all the events and preparations surrounding us, this is probably the busiest, most rushed time of the year. The church invites us to take the slower time, to find ways to live in the present moment, deepening and understanding the gift we have been given.

Materials
- ☐ 24 (or so) envelopes for each child/youth
- ☐ Copies of the handout
- ☐ Blank slips of paper
- ☐ Scissors
- ☐ Pencils, markers

Lesson Starter
Ask: ***What did your family do during the days before Christmas last year, the days of Advent?***

Acknowledge the busy schedules of the season; then share with your learners the church's invitation to make Advent a slower time, a time of rituals that bring us closer to Jesus and to one another, including our family.

Share with the children/youth that many families have rituals during the Advent season to celebrate the meaning of the season and to spend time with each other. Ask: ***What are some things that families might do during the Advent season?***

Activity
Invite the children/youth to think of and choose what they would like their family to do during this Advent season to remember Jesus. They can cut out ideas from the handout, or write down ideas that were suggested by the group or other ideas that come to them.

Place each one in a separate envelope, dating the outside of the envelope. A few of the activities are designed for a specific date; the others can be determined by the children/youth. They might want to decorate the envelopes.

Invite the children/youth to take the envelopes home. Suggest placing them on their family dinner table, opening one each evening and discussing as a family how they might do the suggested activity.

Prayer Together
Emmanuel, God with us in every moment, during this Advent season slow us down. As we celebrate the coming of your Son, Jesus, deepen our caring within our families and our reaching out to all in our human family.

Options
- Prior to this session communicate with the parents, asking for activities their families have done in the past and what they might like to do this year. Add these into your discussion with your learners.
- Instead of envelopes, these ideas might be placed on an Advent Chain. One of the advantages of the envelopes is the experience of waiting—an Advent theme—to discover what suggestion is in each envelope.

Make an Advent Chain to count the days throughout Advent to Christmas.

First Sunday of Advent:
Set up your family Advent wreath.

Make a family trip to the library and check out some books about Christmas.

Go shopping together to buy a new toy for a charitable organization.

Read the Christmas story from the gospels of Matthew and Luke.

Tonight, play Christmas music and make decorations for your tree.

Begin tonight to put up your nativity scene. Talk about the part that each person or animal had in the Christmas story.

Tonight, take a family walk in your neighborhood and look at Christmas decorations.

Tonight is a no-television night. Spend time tonight reading those books you checked out of the library.

Tonight (Dec. 5), get ready for the feast of St. Nicholas by making gift certificates for everyone in the family.

Today (Dec. 6), celebrate the feast of St. Nicholas. Exchange your gift certificates. Telephone a loved one long distance for a surprise.

Today (Dec. 8) is one of the feasts of Mary. As part of your family prayer together, pray the Hail Mary. How do you think Mary felt while she waited for Jesus to be born?

Make a list of love and appreciation. Talk about what you love/appreciate about each person on your list. Be sure to have someone take notes; then give the notes to each person.

Pray together: Thank you, God, for the excitement we feel. It is very hard to wait to find out what will be under the tree. Help us to think more of you. Give us the peace of Christmas as we continue waiting.

Tonight, make a family Christmas card for one of the special people on your list.

Let everyone take a turn telling what she or he thinks was the best thing about last Christmas.

Whoever opens this envelope gets to choose what the family will do together this evening.

Write a prayer together that you can use when you place the Infant Jesus in the crib.

We are getting ready to remember the birth of Jesus. Take out your picture albums and remember the birth of each family member.

Have a wireless evening/day. Unplug everything and decide on a way to just enjoy/be together with your family.

Give someone a simple gift and don't take credit for it. You could leave baked goods, candy, or an anonymous Advent greeting on a neighbor's doorstep.

Read about the Old Testament people that are featured on the Jesse Tree. Make one or two ornaments of Jesse Tree people.

Make cookies for a lonely neighbor, for a soup kitchen, etc.

Decorate a mini-Christmas tree and take it to someone in a nursing home.

Take all of your Christmas books, wrap them, and put them in a box. Each night—or once a week—take one, unwrap it, and read it together.

As a family, record a Christmas voicemail message—in the spirit of the meaning of Christmas.

Pray the O Antiphons before dinner each evening (the week before Christmas).

Offer to babysit for another family so the parents can go shopping.

2 THE **ALTAR**

Objective
To engage the imagination of the learners as they understand that the altar represents Christ and the body of Christ

Background for Catechists
In his general audience on February 5, 2014, Pope Francis, speaking about the Eucharist and the layout of Catholic churches, observed that in the "center...we find the altar," which is "a table that has been prepared and that makes us think of a banquet...."

The *General Instruction of the Roman Missal* (nos. 306–308) reminds us that only what is required for the celebration of Mass is placed on the altar. This includes the Book of the Gospels (at the beginning of Mass, before it is taken to the ambo), the *Roman Missal*, and the chalice with the paten. The candles and crucifix are placed near or on the altar (assuring that they do not interfere with the people's clear view of the eucharistic action on the altar).

Catholic teaching articulates that the altar symbolizes both Jesus Christ and the body of Christ (all of us). The members of the church "are the living stones out of which the Lord Jesus builds the Church's altar" (*Dedication of a Church and an Altar*, no. 2). The design of the altar, then, is an expression of the uniqueness of the community that gathers around it.

Materials
- ☐ Scissors
- ☐ Markers or crayons
- ☐ Copies of the handout

Lesson Starter
Ask: *What is one of your favorite places in your home? When relatives and friends gather in your home, where do they often end up?* (Hopefully, some children/youth will say the dinner/kitchen table.)

Lead the children/youth to realize that a family table, our altar, is in our church home too. Use the information above to describe what is placed on the altar.

Activity
Distribute copies of the handout, along with markers or crayons. Invite the children to draw a picture of the altar in their church. Remind them to include the required elements. Then ask them to draw the people who are present at the altar, along with other details that describe their parish church.

After the children finish, draw them together to share their pictures. Invite them to share about the altar and the celebration of the Mass in the parish.

Prayer Together
Nourishing God, we gather around many tables. At our family table, deepen our care for each other. As we celebrate at your altar, make us more aware of who we are, called to be the body of Christ in our world.

Options
- Engage the children in building an altar, using cardboard boxes or other materials.
- Children/youth might write an explanation of the design of their altar.

The Altar

TABLE OF THE EUCHARIST

Draw a picture of the altar in your parish. Include the important things that are used on the altar. Draw the people who celebrate the Eucharist together.

3 THE **AMBO—TABLE** OF THE **WORD**

Objective
To deepen learning about the importance of the word of God during liturgy, using imagination and creativity

Background for Catechists
The church (especially through the Second Vatican Council) reminds us of the many ways Jesus is present with us during the liturgy. We are fed and nourished through God's word and the Eucharist. The *General Introduction to the Lectionary for Mass* reminds us that there is a close relationship between the altar and the ambo, emphasizing the connection between word and Eucharist: the two tables, the table of the word and the table of the Eucharist.

The U.S. bishops' document *Built of Living Stones* gives further guidance on the use of the ambo: "Our reverence for the word of God is expressed not only in an attentive listening to and reflection upon the Scripture, but also by the way we handle and treat the Book of the Gospels. The ambo can be designed not only for reading and preaching, but also for displaying the open Book of the Gospels or a copy of the Scriptures before and after the liturgical celebration" (no. 62).

Materials
☐ Pencils, markers, crayons
☐ Copies of the handout

Lesson Starter
Ask: *When someone shares an important message* (college classes, the president's State of the Union speech, etc.), *where does the speaker often stand?*

As the learners explore the use of lecterns and podiums, help them to see that the church has a unique kind: an ambo. It's much more than a podium; it's a table from which we are fed, since the message (the word of God) is so crucial to our lives: it leads us to Eucharist, and Eucharist leads us to live the word of God.

Discuss with your learners the uniqueness and reverence due the ambo and the use of the two liturgical books used at the ambo: the lectionary (the book of the readings for each Sunday and weekday Mass as well as for other liturgies: baptism, anointing of the sick, funerals, rites of blessings, etc.) and the Book of the Gospels (gospels for Sundays and feasts of our Lord and the saints). Invite them to imagine what the covers of these two books might look like.

Share with your learners that, at times, churches (following guidelines from *Built of Living Stones*, nos. 126–127) use a simple fabric hanging, a stole-like piece, conveying the color and a symbol or image of the liturgical season.

Activity
Divide your group in half. Invite half of the children/youth to design a front cover for the Book of the Gospels; invite the other half of the group to design a simple hanging for the front of the ambo.

Prayer Together
Word of God, as we gather around the table of the word, open our hearts to cherish your message. Open our lips to share your message. Open our hands and feet to be your message to our world.

Options
- If there is time—or enough children/youth to divide into three groups—invite them to also design a cover for the Lectionary.
- They might design several hangings for the ambo—for each of the liturgical seasons and for celebrations of baptism, confirmation, marriage, etc.

The Ambo
TABLE OF THE WORD

Design a cover for the Book of the Gospels or
a simple hanging for the front of the ambo.

4 BAPTISMAL DAYS

Objective
To enable learners to learn more about the sacrament of baptism, especially their baptismal day, through interviews of people who celebrated the day

Background for Catechists
Baptism, the sacrament of the beginning of new life in Christ, is just that: a beginning. Baptism isn't a once-and-done sacrament. We live our baptism and our baptismal promises each and every day.

One of the ways to keep our focus on the centrality of our baptism is to remember and celebrate the anniversary of our baptism: remembering with our families, reminiscing over photos, bringing out our baptismal candle and baptismal white garment, having a special meal, and praying together, especially renewing our baptismal promises.

Materials
- ☐ Copies of the handout
- ☐ Blank paper
- ☐ Pencils or pens

Lesson Starter
Ask: *Do you remember the day of your baptism?* (Some might say yes because their family has talked about it with them, shown them the pictures, etc.) *Do you know the date of your baptism? Who was there with you? Why did your parents have you baptized?*

Talk with your children/youth about the importance of baptism in our lives: initiation into the Christian community, the bestowal of a name (our personal name and the name "Christian"), renunciation of sin, the celebration that God has chosen us, the gift of grace, and the beginning of a new life in Jesus Christ.

Activity
Invite your children/youth to interview some people who were present at their baptism (their parents, godparents, grandparents, other relatives and friends, etc.). (Interviewing is a helpful catechetical activity that involves family members/others in the community in the child's faith formation, helps the children/youth benefit from the wisdom of the larger community, and helps the learners to connect their classroom learning with the "real" world.)

Distribute copies of the handout and use it to help your learners prepare for the interview. Distribute blank paper and invite the children to write down some questions to ask for their interview. Then draw them together to discuss some of their questions. Encourage them to use the papers as they conduct their interview.

Provide time in subsequent sessions for the children/youth to share their findings with the rest of the group. Invite them too to share all that they found out with their parents.

Prayer Together
God of New Life, in baptism we were signed with the cross, immersed in the saving waters, and anointed with holy oil. You call us by name, calling us to grow in wisdom, age, and grace. We promise to walk with others in your love, to care for others, and to be peacemakers in our world.

Options
- Invite the learners to create something to help them remember all that they have discovered: a booklet, a PowerPoint, a poster, etc., about their baptism.
- Encourage families to celebrate the baptismal anniversaries of every family member.

Interviews about My Baptismal Day

A Few Interview Pointers

Make a list of the people you will interview. Your parents can help by telling you who was present.

What kinds of questions will help these people share their experiences with you?

Write your questions down and decide on a logical order for the interview.

Go to the interview prepared to jot down the answers. (You might want to ask the person if you could record them.)

Listen carefully to each answer. Sometimes the answer will tell you what your next question should be.

Look at the person when she or he is talking with you.

Even though you write down or record the answers, don't concentrate so much on getting the information that you don't really listen to what the person is saying.

At the end of the interview, thank the person for talking with you.

Afterward, let the persons you interviewed know how your report went with the group—how it helped them and you.

Some Suggested Questions to Ask

1   What was I like on the day of my baptism?

2   Is there one thing you especially remember about the celebration of the rite when I was baptized?

3   How did you feel during the celebration of my baptism? Did it remind you of anything?

4   Did you make the sign of the cross on my forehead? How did you feel when you did that?

5   Do you remember the message of the homily?

6   Was I baptized by immersion or by pouring of the water?

7   (Parents): Why did you have me baptized?

8   When and where were you baptized? Do you know who was there with you? Do you celebrate the anniversary of your baptism?

9   What does the sacrament of baptism mean to you?

10 How do you live your baptismal promises today?

5 CATHOLIC SOCIAL TEACHING

Objective
To gain a deeper understanding of Catholic Social Teaching, applying it to everyday situations

Background for Catechists
In reality, Catholic Social Teaching is very old. Throughout the church's history, the church has always talked about and acted on issues of our social life—our life with each other—following the teachings of Jesus. Often, however, the term "Catholic Social Teaching" refers to documents from the popes, the Second Vatican Council, and the bishops that have been written within the last 120 years.

These documents and exhortations address various areas of our life together, including the political, economic, social, and cultural. They talk about current realities in the lives of people and societies, highlighting the benefits and dangers in those realities that affect the dignity and rights of all people.

Several years ago, the U.S. bishops named seven key themes that are at the heart of our tradition of Catholic Social Teaching. (See the handout summarizing the themes in language that children/youth can understand.)

Materials
- ☐ Copies of handout
- ☐ Internet access
- ☐ Newspapers, magazines
- ☐ Sunday bulletins
- ☐ Pencils, paper

Lesson Starter
Ask: *Are there people in your life* (parents, teachers, grandparents, godparents, etc.) *who help you understand what is happening in your life, in the world around you? Who help you to understand the advantages and the pitfalls of your attitudes and actions?*

As a church, we are fortunate because that happens for us too.

Explain in a simple fashion the body of Catholic Social Teaching within the church and the seven key themes.

Activity
Divide your learners into seven groups. Give each group one of the themes of Catholic Social Teaching. Invite them to search the Internet, magazines, newspapers, Sunday bulletins, etc., looking for articles, pictures, and words that illustrate their theme.

After they have collected a wide variety of words, pictures, and articles, invite them to design a television documentary about their theme. Encourage their creativity. In addition to the "script," they might wish to use Power-Point, posters, visuals, songs, interviews, etc.

Prayer Together
Jesus, Light of the World, help us to bring light to your world. Jesus, who sought out those who were hurting, help us to bring care to your world. Jesus, Prince of Peace, help us to be peacemakers in your world.

Options
- ■ Invite your learners to write letters to TV stations, newspapers, legislators, and others about their theme of Catholic Social Teaching. Even small children can understand and write about many of the issues, such as peace, respect for creation, and caring for the needy.

The Seven Themes of Catholic Social Teaching

The dignity of the human person

- All people are holy, made in the image of God.

- God made every one of us. We are called to treat others with great respect and fairness because God made them too.

We are called to live as family and community

- People are both holy and social; when one suffers, we all suffer.

- We, as humans, need to be around other people to be happy and healthy. Jesus wants us to live in families, have friends and neighbors, and also care for one another.

Rights and responsibilities

- Every person needs food, work, a home, school, and medical care in order to live. Every person has a right to have these.

- When some people don't have these things, it is our responsibility to help them obtain their rights.

An option for the poor and vulnerable

- The gospel test of a community (or society) is how it treats those in need.

- Some people do not have what is necessary to live: food, water, work, housing, school, and medical care. They are considered poor. Our church teaches that these brothers and sisters must be treated with extra respect and extra care and given what they need.

The dignity and rights of workers

- Money, work, and business exist to serve people, not the other way around.

- Work gives us the means to live, giving us a chance to use the talents God gives us. Through our work, we are helping God create our world. Because everyone is created by God, workers deserve to have safe conditions, reasonable hours, and fair wages.

Solidarity

- We are called to work for justice for all people.

- The people of the world need each other, and we must work together if we are to live. When we share our lives with others around the world, we become the best we can be. Despite differences, we are one family—the family of God.

We are called to stewardship

- The earth and all life on it is God's creation. When we use the earth's resources unwisely, many people suffer.

- Making wise choices is called "good stewardship."

6 THE **CROSS**

Objective
To deepen understanding of the symbol of the cross

Background for Catechists
The cross is one of the earliest and most widely used Christian symbols. It illuminates a core belief of the Christian faith: Jesus died on the cross and was raised from the dead. Even though it was the means of execution for criminals at the time of Jesus, it is now a sign of victory over death and suffering.

Throughout history, a great variety of crosses have developed, some with specific symbolic meaning and others that are associated with various groups or nationalities.

The cross has been used in paintings, statues, church decorations, and jewelry throughout the history of Christianity. We especially use the cross in physical gestures, as we make the sign of the cross in prayer, remembering our baptism and our following of Christ.

Materials
- ☐ Copies of handout
- ☐ Books with examples of various crosses
- ☐ Printed pages from the Internet for each cross (*You might ask parents or teens in your parish to prepare this information.*)
- ☐ Pencils, markers, and crayons
- ☐ Poster boards or large construction paper
- ☐ 5 x 8 cards
- ☐ Paint and clay

Lesson Starter
Ask: *Have you ever belonged to a club that had a symbol by which everyone knew who you were, the purpose of your group?*

We belong to the Christian family. Is there a sign or symbol that reminds us and others that we are Jesus' followers?

Explain that, throughout history, the cross has always pointed to the identity of Christians, but the symbol of the cross has been expressed in various ways —each telling us a little something about our beliefs.

Activity
Distribute copies of the handout. Invite each learner to choose one or more of the crosses. In the space next to the crosses, have them write what they think the cross symbolizes, based on its title or shape. Then invite them to design their own cross in the frame. This additional cross should be their original design. How would their cross illustrate something they believe about Jesus or about our faith? Gather the group together and invite them to share their responses and their own cross designs.

Options
- Invite students to research the various crosses on the handout and bring the results to the next session.
- Have them make a cross poster and display it by the prayer table.

Prayer Together
We adore you, O Christ, and we bless you, because by your holy cross you have redeemed the world.

Options
- The learners could be given only the names of the crosses; they would research the meaning and image.
- Invite your children/youth to create a cross that incorporates symbols of their community.

CELTIC CROSS

JERUSALEM CROSS

BUDDED CROSS

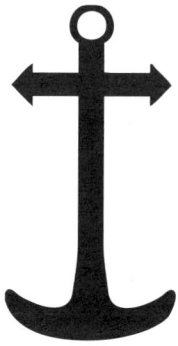

ANCHOR CROSS

ST. PETER'S CROSS

PATRIARCHAL CROSS

CALVARY CROSS

7 **FAITH SHARING**

Objective

To participate in an enriching faith practice of the church: faith sharing

Background for Catechists

The *General Directory for Catechesis* underlines the importance of the group as one of the elements of catechetical methodology: "Groups are practically a vital necessity for personality formation…they promote a sense of dialogue and sharing as well as a sense of Christian co-responsibility" (no. 159).

Throughout our Catholic history, one of the helpful faith practices that has enabled people to grow is listening to and sharing faith experiences, thoughts, and feelings. Faith sharing broadens us, suggests fresh ways of thinking, and stretches us to consider things that we might have missed or never thought about. In our sharing with others, the verbalization of our experiences, thoughts, and feelings concretizes them for us; in the telling, we are often led to understand our experiences in new ways.

Materials

☐ The handout questions can be used by the catechist to suggest possible starters.

Lesson Starter

Ask: *What do you talk about with your friends? Does talking with and listening to friends help you understand things in a new way?*

This happens to us as Christians too. Our faith is not just between me and God. Faith is lived and shared. St. Paul says, "Faith comes from what is heard" (Romans 10:17). When we listen to others, when we listen to ourselves say something aloud, we see our faith in new ways, we might understand something from a different perspective, and we marvel at how God lives with us.

Activity

Often throughout your sessions, invite children/youth to faith sharing. Some guidelines:

- Faith sharing is often best done in small groups, usually two or three people.
- Sharing one's faith with another is a great gift, and the one who receives is in the midst of an awe-filled experience. Therefore, what is shared within that small group stays within the small group.
- The small group needs some direction: a question or open-ended sentence that flows from Scripture, the theme of the session, etc. Catechists can phrase these according to the age and needs of the group.
- Faith sharing is not a time to give advice; it is a time for each person to listen to the experiences of the others.
- It's perfectly acceptable not to share. The goal is to enable children/youth to become comfortable with faith sharing, but on a particular day or with a particular topic, someone might not be able to talk. That is perfectly all right.

The handout suggests some faith-sharing starters related to children's/youth's experiences of God. Similar questions and open-ended sentences can be designed for any theme/topic.

Prayer Together

Listening God, may our prayerful listening to each other help us to recognize you everywhere, sharing your story and your care with everyone we meet.

Option

Send the handout home with the children and suggest that families use it for sharing faith among themselves.

Faith-Sharing Starters about God

- What color reminds you of God?

- How does it make you feel when someone tells you that you are a child of God?

- Do you know any people who love God? How can you tell they love God?

- What does God sound like?

- What if God whispered to you right now? What would God say?

- What happened to you last week that reminded you of God?

- Do you ask God things? What things? Does God ask you things? What things?

- If you sang a song to God, what song would you sing?

- If God gave you a compliment, what would it be?

- If you asked God to teach you to pray, what would God say?

- Where do you pray best? Why?

- What advertising slogan would be a good description of God?

- Finish this sentence: "If my relationship with God was the basis for a TV show, I'd call it _____."

- What if you could ask God to solve one problem in the world?

- Finish this sentence: The person that most easily influences me to believe in God or at least to think about God is _____.

Faith-Sharing Starters about God for Families

- Gather the family together to read the newspaper. Which news stories show God's presence and care in the world?

- What's your favorite adjective for God?

- How has God blessed our family?

- I wonder what would make our family feel like shouting Alleluia.

- If God had one sentence to say to our family, I think it would be _____.

- I think God is _____.

- The Bible says we are created in the image of God. How do you image, look like, or act like God?

- The place where I like to pray to God is _____.

- Our home is God's home because _____.

- (Saying to each other family member) "I think the thing that God likes most about you is _____."

- Finish this sentence: "I think the thing God likes most about our family is _____."

- Finish this sentence: "I felt God was especially with our family when _____."

- What gifts does God give us that we can't touch or see?

- Go on a walk together and look for great and small things that God has made. Have everyone find one small thing that she or he can take home. Work together and make a table centerpiece out of small things God has made.

8 FEASTS OF MARY, THE MOTHER OF GOD

Objective

To deepen awareness of the role of Mary in our Catholic life; to become familiar with some of the church's Marian feasts

Background for Catechists

We, as Catholics, have a special devotion to Mary, the Mother of God, the first disciple. This devotion to Mary is manifested in prayer, the visual arts, poetry, and music.

Many Marian feasts occur throughout the liturgical year. Some celebrate events in Mary's life; others recognize Mary's intercession and involvement in our lives.

Materials

- ☐ Paper
- ☐ Pencils
- ☐ Copies of the handout
- ☐ Student text: lessons on Mary
- ☐ Books of church feast days, especially Marian feasts
- ☐ Internet access to Marian feasts (or pages you have printed)

Lesson Starter

Ask: *Are there times throughout the year when your family celebrates you in a special way? What are they remembering and celebrating? Why do you think they do that?*

Are there any days throughout the year when people celebrate their mothers in special ways? How? Why?

Remind the learners that as members of the family of God, we remember and celebrate Mary, Mother of Jesus, and model for us. Just as we celebrate our specialness—and the specialness of moms—through birthdays and Mother's Day, etc., we remember the unique-ness of Mary throughout our liturgical year. Each feast day tells us something about Mary.

Activity

Music is an enjoyable and powerful method to learn, to imagine, and to remember.

Invite the children/youth to form groups of two or three.

As we think about—and remember—Mary and her many feasts, invite each group to choose a popular melody (e.g., "The twelve days of Christmas") and then write a new song about one of the Marian feasts, telling just a little bit about the meaning of the feast.

To research the feasts, they can use their own textbooks, books from the parish library, or Internet sites on Marian feasts.

Take time, of course, to hear each group's musical creation.

Prayer Together

My soul magnifies the Lord, and my spirit rejoices in God my Savior; because he has regarded the lowliness of his handmaid; for behold, henceforth all generations shall call me blessed; because he who is mighty has done great things for me, and holy is his name; and his mercy is from generation to generation on those who fear him. He has shown might with his arm; he has scattered the proud in the conceit of their hearts. He has put down the mighty from their thrones, and has exalted the lowly. He has filled the hungry with good things, and the rich he has sent away empty. He has given help to Israel, his servant, mindful of his mercy, even as he spoke to our fathers, to Abraham and to his posterity forever. (LUKE 1:46–55)

Options

- Invite the children to use the handout to research different Marian feasts.
- The songs could be used periodically during prayer, especially on or near a Marian feast.

Some of the Marian Feasts Celebrated in our Church

JANUARY 1
Mary, the Holy Mother of God

FEBRUARY 2
Presentation of the Lord

FEBRUARY 11
Our Lady of Lourdes

MARCH 25
The Annunciation of the Lord

APRIL 26
Our Lady of Good Counsel

MAY 13
Our Lady of Fatima

MAY 31
The Visitation of the
Blessed Virgin Mary

JUNE 27
Our Mother of Perpetual Help

JULY 16
Our Lady of Mount Carmel

AUGUST 15
The Assumption of the
Blessed Virgin Mary

AUGUST 22
The Queenship of the
Blessed Virgin Mary

SEPTEMBER 8
Nativity of the Blessed Virgin Mary

SEPTEMBER 12
The Most Holy Name of Mary

SEPTEMBER 15
Our Lady of Sorrows

OCTOBER 7
Our Lady of the Rosary

NOVEMBER 21
Presentation of the
Blessed Virgin Mary

DECEMBER 8
The Immaculate Conception

9 THE **FRUITS** OF THE **HOLY SPIRIT**

Objective
To imagine ways that the fruits of the Holy Spirit are lived in everyday life

Background for Catechists
We are gifted—at baptism and confirmation—with the seven gifts of the Holy Spirit. When we are guided by these gifts, our lives generate specific characteristics: the fruits of the Holy Spirit. Just as a tree produces fruit when properly nourished and cared for, people who develop the Spirit's gifts show concrete evidence of their faithfulness.

Scripture (Galatians 5:22–23) lists nine fruits: love, joy, peace, patience, kindness, goodness, faithfulness, gentleness, self-control. The *Catechism of the Catholic Church* delineates twelve: "charity, joy, peace, patience, kindness, goodness, generosity, gentleness, faithfulness, modesty, self-control, chastity" (no. 1832).

Materials
- ☐ A bowl of fruit
- ☐ A large bowl with several slips of paper, each containing the name of one of the fruits of the Holy Spirit.
- ☐ A bowl containing slips of paper listing movie or TV genres (e.g., news show, action movie, commercial, history, adventure, musicals, fantasy, documentary, game shows, animated shows, court show, hidden camera, interview, talk show, variety show)
- ☐ Copies of the handout

Lesson Starter
As the children/youth look at the bowl of varied fruit (invite them to enjoy a piece), ask:
What enabled these fruits to grow?

Because of the many gifts of God (rain, sun, nutrients in the soil, etc.), each plant/vine/ tree produced delicious fruit. The same is true for us. The Holy Spirit gives us gifts (wisdom, understanding, right judgment, courage, knowledge, reverence, wonder and awe). These gifts enable us to live good, holy lives. Because of them, we are able—with the Spirit's guidance—to produce loving actions, to bring forth wonderful fruit: the fruits of the Holy Spirit in all the aspects of our lives.

Activity
Form groups of three or four. Have each group draw one slip of paper from each bowl. Using the handout—and your discussions—invite each group to talk further about the actions associated with their fruit.

Invite them to create a skit to explain and give practical actions that illustrate their fruit, using the movie or TV genre they also draw.

Invite the groups to present their skits one at a time. If there is not time for everyone to present in one session, one group could present at each subsequent session, thereby keeping the theme of living the fruits always before the learners.

Prayer Together
Holy Spirit, you are generous in responding to our needs. Teach us generosity. Holy Spirit, you reveal the faithfulness of God. Draw us to live more faithfully with you.

Option
Invite the learners to write a "review" of each skit—but not about the performance or the quality of the skit; the review would be about the fruit: its advantages in our Catholic life, the challenges as we live that fruit, etc.

The Fruits of the Holy Spirit

Charity/Love: This fruit especially shines forth when we reach out to those around us and beyond us who are in need, including the poor, the sick, or victims of injustice. We are constantly concerned about the needs of others.

Joy: Joy is beyond happiness. We can be happy when we eat a good dinner. A joyful person celebrates life, even in the midst of pain and confusion, because of a deep relationship with God.

Peace: Peace is having a restful relationship with God. Life becomes less worrisome because we know God is present in the good times and the bad; we realize that God never leaves.

Patience: Knowing we are truly loved, we can endure hardships, suffering, and the insensitivity of other people. We let the moments of distress pass.

Kindness: Kindness is showing concern for those in need, through actions or words of encouragement.

Goodness: Because of God's great love, we desire to always do what we know is right, loving everyone without exception and working for everything that is good for them.

Generosity: We live generously when we share our gifts, time, and possessions with others. At times it might mean we have to sacrifice something, but the needs of others are our first concern.

Gentleness: Gentle people act calmly and avoid actions that might lead others to anger or resentment.

Faith/Fidelity: We are faithful when we live out our commitment to the teachings of Jesus, the Scriptures, and the Catholic Church. Because of our faith relationship with God, we also have faith in—a deep trust in—people.

Modesty: We exhibit modesty through balance, fairness, and discipline in all our actions, especially our conversations and behaviors. Modesty is a sign that we give God credit for our talents and successes.

Self-Control: We are self-controlled when we work to overcome the temptations we face and we try always to do God's will.

Chastity: Because of chastity, we form loving and caring friendships, which help us to act appropriately with our gift of sexuality.

10 GESTURES IN PRAYER

Objective
To learn more about the importance of gesture in prayer, especially by designing prayerful gestures

Background for Catechists
Throughout the ages, the church has used many gestures in prayer, which reminds us that prayer is not just words; our whole bodies pray. The website of the U.S. bishops explains: "In the celebration of Mass we raise our hearts and minds to God. We are creatures of body as well as spirit, so our prayer is not confined to our minds and hearts. It is expressed by our bodies as well. When our bodies are engaged in our prayer, we pray with our whole person. Using our entire being in prayer helps us to pray with greater attentiveness."

Some of the gestures used during liturgy and sacraments:

- The sign of the cross
- Using holy water as we enter and leave church
- Bowing from the waist
- Bowing the head
- Genuflecting
- Striking of the breast
- Standing, kneeling, sitting
- Making the sign of the cross on our foreheads and lips, and over our hearts
- The sign of peace
- Laying on of hands
- Washing of the feet

Materials
☐ Copies of the handout
☐ Bibles

Lesson Starter
Ask: *How do we use gestures in everyday life* (wave, handshake, nod of the head, hug, etc.)?

Why do we use them? What do they "say"? Do you think they are important? Helpful?

Help the children/youth to review some of the gestures we use in liturgy, and to see that gestures, at times, can take the place of words; at other times, gestures intensify our words, making very explicit our feelings and thoughts.

During our personal prayer and group prayer (outside of our liturgical prayer), we can also use gestures: gestures from our liturgy, other gestures that we might even make up that convey our thoughts and feelings, and, at times, sign language. Using all these gestures will enhance our prayer and make us more attentive to the gestures we use in liturgy.

Activity
Invite small groups of children to design gestures for each line of a prayer. Invite each group to use a different prayer: Our Father, Hail Mary, a prayer they have written, one of the psalms, or a liturgical song.

The gestures on the handout are only some of many possible gestures; at times, the same gesture might also mean different things.

Prayer Together
Glory be to the Father, and to the Son,
    and to the Holy Spirit. (BOW HEADS)
As it was in the beginning, (STRETCH ARMS
    FORWARD, POINTING TO THE EARTH)
is now, and ever shall be, (RAISE ARMS ABOVE HEAD)
world without end. (BRING ARMS IN FRONT IN A
    CIRCLE AS IF YOU WERE CIRCLING THE EARTH)
Amen. (FOLD HANDS IN PRAYER)

Option
Have the small groups teach their prayer and gestures to another group of learners, perhaps a grade or two younger than they are.

Some Prayerful Gestures

Hands uplifted and extended outward

(gesture of asking)

Arms crossed over the chest

(sign of drawing something/someone close to us)

Arms raised upward

(sign of praise)

Hands folded

(gesture of drawing our whole body into prayer or of being united with God)

Hands joined with others

(gesture of unity)

Palms up

(gesture of asking)

One hand holding the other with both palms up

(gesture of offering ourselves)

Head bowed

(gesture of meditation or humility)

Head lifted up

(gesture of openness, anticipation, receptivity)

Arms outstretched

(gesture of petition)

Standing attentive

(gesture of waiting, receptivity, readiness)

Eyes closed

(gesture of meditation, reflection)

Eyes looking upward

(sign of anticipation, expectation, longing)

HOLY DAYS AND FEASTS

Objective

To become aware of, as well as make plans for celebrating, some of our Catholic holy days and feasts

Background for Catechists

Catholics in the U.S. celebrate six holy days of obligation in addition to Sundays: All Saints (November 1), Christmas (December 25), Mary, the Mother of God (January 1), Ascension Thursday (when not moved to the following Sunday), Assumption of Mary (August 15), and the Immaculate Conception (December 8). In addition, on many days of the year, we remember one (sometimes more than one) saint or holy person from throughout the ages.

Materials

- ☐ Copies of handout
- ☐ Books of feast days
- ☐ Articles on significant feasts and holy days printed from the web
- ☐ Pencils

Lesson Starter

Say: *Are there some days in the year* (in this month) *that stand out for you, or are a little bit different than the others? Your birthday or Christmas or Halloween might come to your mind. We are fortunate; in many ways each day is different; each has just a little different flavor. We often remember events that have happened throughout history (July 4) or days that have been designated for a specific awareness (Earth Day on April 22, International Day of Peace on September 21). As Catholics, each day, we remember someone from our past who is part of our family. We have a Catholic calendar of holy days and feasts.*

Activity

Divide your group into smaller groups of six or twelve; if twelve, each group is given one month; if six, each group has two months. (Or if you have twelve learners, each could work alone on one month.)

Using the various books or articles, invite the children/youth to fill in their calendar(s) with some of the holy days/feasts for each month, and to find an action that flows from the feast that might be done by themselves or with their families.

For instance:

- In the spirit of St. Nicholas (December 6), prepare some "sacks of gold" (a few Christmas cookies or candies in a bag with ribbon). Leave the bags for others anonymously.
- On the feast of St. Kateri Tekakwitha (patron of the environment and ecology) on July 14, pick up any litter we see around our neighborhood.

Copies of each month's calendar can be made and sent home for family use. Keep a copy in your meeting space to recall the upcoming days during prayer and decision-making time.

Prayer Together

Holy God, because of you, all our days are holy. We celebrate the specialness of each day, remembering the women and men who have gone before us who model for us living in the holy present moment, the moments of your grace.

Option

Rather than a calendar for the whole year at once, each month might be done by everyone just before the month begins.

Holy Days and Feasts

[MONTH]

SUNDAY	MONDAY	TUESDAY	WEDNESDAY	THURSDAY	FRIDAY	SATURDAY

12 JESUS

Objective
To learn about some of the symbols the church uses for Jesus; to create a new symbol that expresses each learner's thoughts about Jesus

Background for Catechists
As we talk about various symbols (and practices and traditions) within our faith, one of our core "symbols" is certainly Jesus. Jesus is the ultimate symbol of God; because of Jesus—his life, his teachings, his values, and his witness—we know God in a unique and real way.

Throughout our history—beginning with Scripture—many and varied symbols and names have been used for Jesus. Each one of them gives us another view of Jesus, another lens through which to understand who he is and all that he does.

Materials
- ☐ Copies of handout
- ☐ Bibles
- ☐ Blank paper
- ☐ Markers or crayons

Lesson Starter
Share with your learners that sometimes people use symbols to describe some aspect of their lives. Name examples, such as poppies for war veterans, an apple for a teacher, a tractor or sheaves of wheat for a farmer, or a heart to illustrate care.

Distribute the handout. Introduce the children/youth to the many different symbols for Jesus. Explain that some of them were used to describe Jesus in Scripture. As you explore the symbols on the handout, invite your learners to tell about other symbols they have seen.

Activity
Invite children/youth to reflect on Jesus in their lives. Who is Jesus for them? What symbol would they use to tell about Jesus? It can't be one that the church already uses; it needs to be unique and new, telling about their own thoughts about Jesus.

Distribute paper and markers. Invite the children/youth to make their own symbol for Jesus. Remind them it does not need to be a work of art. The purpose is to use imagination to perhaps think of Jesus in a new way, in a deeper way, and express that for themselves.

Gather the group together and invite volunteers to share their symbol.

Prayer Together
Jesus, Light of the World, show us the way. Jesus, the Good Shepherd, guide us in your love. Jesus, the True Vine, keep us connected to you. Jesus, Bread of Life, nourish us.

Option
Use clay or no-cook playdough for the symbols. Here is how to make the playdough: 1½ cups flour, 1 cup salt, 2 tablespoons vegetable oil, 1/2 cup water, food coloring. Mix the flour and salt. Slowly add the water and knead to make smooth dough. Add the oil and food coloring and knead until the color is mixed in. No cooking is needed.

Symbols Used for Jesus

The Vine
(JOHN 15:5)

Lamb of God
(JOHN 1:29, 36)

Light
(JOHN 8:12; 9:5)

Bread of Life
(JOHN 6:35)

Good Shepherd
(JOHN 10:11, 14)

King
(LUKE 19:38)

Fish

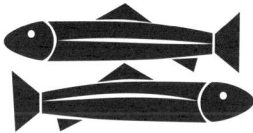

Chi-Ro

IHS

The Pelican

Cornerstone
(EPHESIANS 2:20)

Day Star
(2 PETER 1:19)

The Gate
(JOHN 10:9)

Alpha and Omega
(REVELATION 1:8)

MY SYMBOL FOR JESUS

13 KEEPING THE SABBATH

Objective

To realize anew the importance of Sunday as a day of prayer, rest, joy, and service, and to intentionally plan for family Sundays

Background for Catechists

In 1998, Pope John Paul II wrote *Dies Domini*, an apostolic letter on the sabbath, the day of the Lord. He begins: "The Lord's Day—as Sunday was called from Apostolic times—has always been accorded special attention in the history of the Church because of its close connection with the very core of the Christian mystery" (no. 1).

In addition to affirming the importance of the celebration of liturgy each Sunday, Pope John Paul II reminds us that Sunday is a day of joy, rest, and solidarity. The entire day of Sunday is a sacred time; the events and happenings of our Sundays should be very different from those on our other six days.

Materials

- ☐ Copies of handout
- ☐ Scissors
- ☐ White boxes for each child/youth (could be purchased from bakeries or candy stores)
- ☐ Markers and crayons
- ☐ Pencils
- ☐ Blank strips of paper

Lesson Starter

Ask: *Of the seven days of our week, is there one that is a little bit different from the other six?* When the students have realized that it is Sunday, ask: *What makes Sunday different for us who are Christians?* Remind the group of the third commandment: Remember to keep holy the Lord's day.

Explore with the children/youth the realities of the third commandment and our need to set aside specific time for community worship, for rest from our busy days, for time and activities that refresh and reenergize who we really are, and for focusing on Sunday as the day of resurrection.

Brainstorm with the children (listing on the board, poster, or PowerPoint) things that families could do on Sundays for rest, enjoyment, and caring for others.

Activity

Invite children/youth to look over the Sunday ideas on the handout as well as the ones they have brainstormed together. Have them choose the ones that they would like their family to do every Sunday, or periodically on Sundays. Point out the blank boxes at the bottom of the chart. Explain that these are for their own ideas.

Have them cut apart the ones they choose and/or copy ideas from the list on blank strips of paper. Place the ideas in their box.

The outside of the box can be decorated, making it unique for each family. The box is taken home so that each week the family can pull out an idea for their celebration of Sunday.

Prayer Together

God who rested on the seventh day, we consecrate the first day of our week to you. As we pray together, bring us closer to you and each another. As we enjoy life, deepen in us an appreciation of all your gifts. As we reach out to others in care and service, enlarge our hearts for your work.

Option

Rather than using a box, learners might want to place each idea on a separate sheet of paper, assembling them into a book. Families could then write the date(s) and a summary on each page of how they used the idea.

Ideas for Sundays

Go on a picnic: in a nearby park or on your family room floor.

Take a walk as a family. Find one thing in nature that you've never noticed before.

Visit someone whom you know who is in the hospital.

Write letters, thank-you cards, and get-well and thinking-of-you notes.

Make together an "I Am Grateful For..." mobile to hang near your family meal table. Think of things for which you are grateful from the last month.

Invite someone who may be unable to cook for themselves, such as an elderly person or shut-in, to share dinner with your family. Or take dinner to them.

Read together a book that is of interest to everyone in the family.

Update and organize your recent family pictures in a photo album.

Practice—or learn—a skill such as knitting. Make a gift for a friend.

Take out family photo albums from years ago; remember the events.

Play a board game together.

Go to a museum, art gallery, or play.

Make phone calls or write letters to your special friends and loved ones to let them know you're thinking of them.

Have each family member make—or update—a personal scrapbook. Include pictures, important letters, certificates, school or work papers, etc.

Each Sunday, feature a different family member in a "Why I Love You" spotlight. Display a picture or craft of that person in a prominent place for a week. Write a brief history of the member and list all of their qualities and strengths.

Take turns planning your family Sundays.

The person in charge chooses the type and place for food, the activity or outing, and those—in addition to the family—who might be invited.

Tell children stories of when they were little and stories of when Mom or Dad was younger.

Have a family meal, including the favorite foods of each person. Everyone participates in getting it ready.

Invite friends or relatives for dinner.

Plant—work in—the garden.

14 THE **SYMBOLS** OF **LENT**

Objective

To explore some of our church's Lenten symbols, creating learning opportunities for younger children

Background for Catechists

Lent is a penitential season in preparation for the very important holy days of our Christian faith, the Triduum: Holy Thursday, Good Friday, and Easter. Lent was, and still is, a retreat-like time for those preparing to celebrate baptism at the Easter Vigil; today it is also a time for all of us to reflect on and renew our baptismal commitment. In the early church, it was also a time of penance for those in the order of penitents, an early form of the sacrament of penance. Today, all of us are called to conversion through prayer, fasting, and almsgiving. Over the centuries, many symbols have evolved that represent the themes of the season: the centrality of baptism, conversion, repentance, and renewal.

Materials

☐ A table with some of the Lenten symbols (or pictures of them): cross, purple cloth, ashes, thorns, palm branches, water, desert, stations of the cross, etc.
☐ Copies of the handout
☐ Paper, poster board, pencils, pens, crayons, markers

Lesson Starter

Using some of the symbols of Lent on the table (and others), ask:

- *What do you think of when you see this symbol?*
- *During the Lenten season, when and where do we find this symbol?*
- *What does it mean for us as Catholics?*

Activity

Form groups of two (or three) learners. Give each group one of the Lenten symbols. Invite them to create a learning station for younger children—a small place/learning center where younger children can see and touch the symbol, learn about it and its meaning and how and when it is used, and engage in an activity.

To explain the symbol, they could create short, written explanations, pictures, a Power-Point and/or provide the actual symbol.

Some possible activities might include making a list of some almsgiving ideas that each learner and their family could do or providing small pretzels attached to a card, on which is written a Lenten prayer.

Prayer Together

God who always calls us to conversion, guide our parish catechumens and candidates and each of us in these Lenten days. May our Lenten symbols, Scripture, worship, and practices of prayer, fasting, and almsgiving strengthen us as we grow as disciples, as people for others. Amen.

Options

- Set up these learning centers in a space large enough for people to move around. Invite the group of younger children to come and explore. Each group remains with their symbol, answering questions, leading the younger children through their explorations. (The younger children move from station to station.)
- Invite the families of your learners to come (perhaps after Sunday liturgy or the last twenty minutes of one of your sessions) and explore the symbols of Lent through these stations.

Some Lenten Symbols

Ashes
(mortality, sorrow, and penance; acknowledgment of sinfulness, our need for God and for conversion; repentance: turning away from sin and evil)

The Color Purple
(symbolizes the desire for conversion, willingness to repent; connected to the soldiers clothing Jesus in a purple cloak [Mk 15:17–20])

The Desert
GOSPEL OF THE FIRST SUNDAY OF LENT
(going away for prayer and fasting; confronted with temptation)

Water
GOSPEL OF THE FOURTH SUNDAY,
HOLY THURSDAY, EASTER VIGIL
(cleansing; service; new life)

Palm Branches
PALM SUNDAY
(Jesus' entry into Jerusalem; honor and victory)

Thorns
GOOD FRIDAY
(suffering and pain; Jesus' crown of thorns)

The Cross/Crucifix
GOOD FRIDAY
(suffering/pain; Jesus' commitment to a life of love)

Praying Hands
(symbolizes one of the three Lenten practices: prayer)

Fish
(represents the second Lenten practice: fasting, which includes remembering that we can fast from many things, not only meat)

Money Bags
(the third Lenten practice: almsgiving, which includes many ways of giving, not only money)

Stations of the Cross
(remembering Jesus' journey to Calvary)

Pretzels
(Because it was a simple food made of flour, water, and salt, it reminded the early Christians of fasting; the design is arms folded in prayer.)

15 | LITANIES

Objective

To become familiar with some of our church's litanies; to write a group litany

Background for Catechists

Litanies are composed of a series of invocations or intercessions, alternating with brief responses. In group prayer, a litany alternates between a leader and the people.

Psalm 136, with its repeated refrain ("for God's mercy endures forever"), is an ancient biblical litany. The *Lord, have mercy,* the General Intercessions, and the *Lamb of God* are forms of litanies in our liturgy.

Six litanies are approved by the church for public recitation: Litany of the Blessed Virgin, Litany of the Saints, Litany of the Holy Name of Jesus, Litany of the Sacred Heart of Jesus, Litany of the Most Precious Blood of Jesus, and Litany of St. Joseph. There are numerous others that are used for private prayer, and new litanies continue to be composed.

Materials

☐ Bibles
☐ Missalettes
☐ Copies of handout
☐ Paper and pencils

Lesson Starter

Ask: *Do you ever repeat things over and over, for instance when you're trying to convince someone that you need something? When else? We have a prayer form in which we repeat a refrain over and over again.*

Explain to the children/youth the structure and style of litanies. Share with them some of the litanies in our heritage. Invite them to look at Psalm 136, as well as the "Lord, have mercy" and the "Lamb of God" from Mass. Pray the Litany of the Blessed Virgin Mary.

Activity

Invite your learners to write a litany of thanksgiving.

Divide them into several small groups, each with the task of writing three short invocations of thanks that will then be added together to form a group litany. (To call forth more creativity, you might give each group three letters—a, b, and c; d, e, and f; etc. They would then write invocations using these—for instance: "We give you thanks for birds, babies, brownies, and birthdays," or "For colorful coats and cheerful children, we are grateful.")

Decide together on the group response that will occur after each invocation. Some examples: "Loving God, we give you thanks" or "We thank you, Gracious God, today and always."

The prayer could be kept to be prayed often during your sessions, and copies could be made for the children/youth to take home for family prayer.

Prayer Together

Praise the Lord for God is good; for God's mercy endures forever; Who skillfully made the heavens, for God's mercy endures forever; Who spread the earth upon the waters, for God's mercy endures forever. (PSALM 136:1, 5–6)

Options

- The groups might choose to illustrate their invocations, producing posters, PowerPoint, etc.
- Have your group use the litany prayer form to compose other prayers: prayers of sorrow, prayers for special needs, or prayers around special themes (e.g., Bread of Life litany, or a litany for peace).
- Invite your learners to write a litany of the saints, incorporating their favorite saints and their patron saints.

The Litany of the Blessed Virgin Mary

LEADER: Lord, have mercy,
ALL: *Lord, have mercy.*

LEADER: Christ, have mercy,
ALL: *Christ have mercy.*

LEADER: Lord, have mercy,
ALL: *Lord, have mercy*

God, the Father of Heaven:
Have mercy on us.
(REPEAT AT END OF EACH PHRASE.)

God, the Son,
  Redeemer of the world,
God, the Holy Spirit,
Holy Trinity, One God,

Holy Mary, **Pray for us**.
(REPEAT AT END OF EACH PHRASE.)

Holy Mother of God,
Holy Virgin of virgins,
Mother of Christ,
Mother of divine grace,
Mother most pure,
Mother most chaste,
Mother inviolate,
Mother undefiled,
Mother most amiable,
Mother most admirable,
Mother of good counsel,
Mother of our Creator,
Mother of our Savior,
Virgin most prudent,
Virgin most venerable,

Virgin most renowned,
Virgin most powerful,
Virgin most merciful,
Virgin most faithful,
Mirror of justice,
Seat of wisdom,
Cause of our joy,
Spiritual vessel,
Vessel of honor,
Singular vessel of devotion,
Mystical rose,
Tower of David,
Tower of ivory,
House of gold,
Ark of the covenant,
Gate of Heaven,
Morning star,
Health of the sick,
Refuge of sinners,
Comforter of the afflicted,
Help of Christians,
Queen of Angels,
Queen of Patriarchs,
Queen of Prophets,
Queen of Apostles,
Queen of Martyrs,
Queen of Confessors,
Queen of Virgins,
Queen of all Saints,
Queen conceived without
  Original Sin,
Queen assumed into Heaven,
Queen of the Most
  Holy Rosary,
Queen of Peace

LEADER: Lamb of God,
who takes away the
sins of the world,

ALL: *Spare us, O Lord.*

LEADER: Lamb of God,
who takes away the
sins of the world,

ALL: *Graciously hear
us, O Lord.*

LEADER: Lamb of God,
who takes away the
sins of the world,

ALL: *Have mercy on us.*

LEADER: Pray for us, O
holy Mother of God.

ALL: *That we may be
made worthy of the
promises of Christ.*

LEADER: Let us pray: Grant,
we beseech you, almighty
God, that we, your faithful,
who rejoice in the name and
under the protection of the
most holy Virgin Mary, may,
by her loving intercession,
be delivered from all evils
here on earth and be made
worthy to reach eternal
glory in the life to come.
Through Christ our Lord.

ALL: *Amen.*

MEALTIME AND BEDTIME PRAYER

Objective
To think of ideas—and make reminders—for prayer at home before mealtimes and before bedtime

Background for Catechists
We realize that there are many ways and many times to pray. Throughout our history, and for many people, two natural times for prayer are before (and after) meals and before bedtime.

Materials
- ☐ Tongue depressors
- ☐ Thin-tip markers
- ☐ Pencils, pens
- ☐ Small stickers
- ☐ Two jars

Lesson Starter
Say: *When do you like to talk with your friends? Anytime is good, isn't it? Sometimes, though, we have special times that seem just right for conversations with our friends. One of the things we know about prayer is that it is talking/listening between God and ourselves. For many people it is important and helpful to take this prayerful time with God before meals and before going to bed each night.*

Ask your learners to share their ways of praying before meals and at bedtime.

Activity
Ask your learners to think about and discuss together:
- Before mealtimes, what might be some things to say "thank you" to God for?
- At the end of the day, what might be some things to say "thank you" to God for?
- Before mealtimes, what might be some petitions, things to ask for?
- At the end of the day, what might be some petitions, things to ask for?

Invite your children/youth to make Prayer Reminder Sticks. Ask them to choose one of the times: mealtimes or bedtime. On one side of the stick, indicate things to thank God for. On the other side, indicate things to talk with God about, to ask God's help with, before meals or before bedtime. These things can be indicated by pasting on small stickers, drawing small pictures, writing a word or phrase, or using a combination of these options.

Place the sticks into two jars: one for mealtime, one for bedtime. Each week, each learner takes one of the sticks (and returns it the following week). As they pray at home, they (and their families) can use the ideas on the stick to form their prayer.

Make copies of the parent letter and send it home as a way to encourage family prayer.

Prayer Together
God with us, we thank you for your amazing, astonishing gifts. We ask your strength for the many people in our lives: our family and friends, all those we meet each day. We ask your help for the happenings of each day, your support as we go through the ups and downs, always living as followers of Jesus.

Options
- Prepare the sticks by drilling/punching a small hole near one end. The children/youth can attach a loop of yarn through the hole (easier to carry/hold on to): one color yarn for mealtime, another color for bedtime.
- You might make the Prayer Reminder Sticks for specific liturgical seasons.

Dear Parents,

Today, as we talked about prayer, we explored the reality that two of people's favorite ways—and times—of praying are before (and after) meals and before going to bed. At times, these prayers can be "memorized prayers"—prayers that everyone knows and can pray together; at other times they can be "spontaneous prayers"—prayers that are prayed on the spot, coming from the needs and feelings within our hearts, the happenings of our day, and the concerns of the people and our world around us.

During our session, each child/youth made a Prayer Reminder Stick (either for mealtime or for bedtime). One side contains pictures and words reminding us of things for which to be grateful. The other side contains pictures and words depicting things for which we might want to ask God's help.

Each week, your child/youth will bring home a different Prayer Reminder Stick. You might want to keep it on your family table, in a visible place in your child's room, on the refrigerator, etc.—a place where everyone will see it every day and use it to spark ideas and thoughts for your family prayer (mealtime or bedtime) each day.

Feel free, too, to use various forms of prayer:
- Silence
- Reading a Scripture story
- Song
- Praying the responsorial psalm from Sunday's liturgy
- Blessing prayers
- A litany of forgiveness
- Sharing the sign of peace
- Search the Internet and/or the parish library for books of mealtime and bedtime prayer

Please help your child/youth remember to return the Reminder Stick each week; she or he will then bring home a new one that, hopefully, will trigger new thoughts for prayer.

Blessings on your days, rooted in prayer,

17 O ANTIPHONS

Objective
To learn about the church's prayer practice of the O Antiphons

Background for Catechists
The week before Christmas is a "season within a season," often referred to as the "Great Advent." Since the seventh century, the O Antiphons have been sung in monasteries all over the world during Vespers for the last seven days of Advent.

Since the Second Vatican Council, the O Antiphons have been adapted (slightly reworded) for the Alleluia Verse before each day's gospel reading. These antiphons are also kept alive for us in our hymn "O Come, O Come, Emmanuel."

Each Antiphon invokes the coming of the Messiah, beginning with a biblical title and closing with a specific petition for God's people, related to the title, and the cry for him to "come."

The seven titles for Jesus in the antiphons are Wisdom, Ruler of the House of Israel (Lord), Root of Jesse, Key of David, Rising Dawn, King of the Nations, and Emmanuel. In Latin the initials of the titles make an acrostic that when read backwards means: "Tomorrow I will be there" ("*Ero cras*").

Materials
- ☐ Copies of handout
- ☐ Bibles
- ☐ Large size of construction paper
- ☐ Pencils
- ☐ Markers and crayons

Lesson Starter
Ask: **Do your family and friends have nicknames for you, or other names that tell something about you?**

Explain to the children/youth that we have many names, or titles, for Jesus, just as we do for people in our lives. During the week before Christmas, the church prays the O Antiphons—short prayers that use several of the (many) titles for Jesus.

Tell them that a custom in the monasteries of old was for different monks to provide treats to the community on these last Advent days—treats/gifts or activities that corresponded with that day's O Antiphon. For instance, the gardener might share his finest fruits when they prayed: "O Root of Jesse...."

Activity
Divide your children/youth into seven groups.

Give each group one of the O Antiphons. Invite each group to divide their construction paper into three sections. Using the handout and the Scripture passages for their O Antiphon:
- Write another prayer in their own words
- Design a symbol
- Think of an activity families could do associated with the O Antiphon; for example, for O Rising Dawn, they might take a drive to see Christmas lights.

Prayer Together
O King of Nations whom all people desire, you are the cornerstone which makes us all one. O come and save us whom you have generously created.

Options
- If this is done prior to December 17, copies (from all seven groups) could be made for each child. They could be assembled into a booklet for them to take home for family prayer in the days preceding Christmas. (Include also the handout.)
- Invite families to make their own O Antiphon symbol each day, making it into an ornament for their Christmas tree.

The O Antiphons

DATE	SCRIPTURE	TITLE	PRAYER OF THE CHURCH	SUGGESTED SYMBOLS
DECEMBER **17**	Sirach 24:2; Wisdom 8:1; Isaiah 11:2–3; 28:29	**O Wisdom**	O Wisdom, you come forth from the mouth of the Most High. You fill the universe and hold all things together in a strong yet gentle manner. O come to teach us the way of truth.	Open book, dove (Holy Spirit), oil lamp
DECEMBER **18**	Exodus 3:2; 20:1; Isaiah 11:4–5; 33:22	**O Lord and Ruler**	O Adonai and Leader of Israel, you appeared to Moses in a burning bush and you gave him the Law on Sinai. O come and save us with your mighty power.	Tablet of the commandments, burning bush
DECEMBER **19**	Isaiah 11:1–3, 10	**O Root of Jesse**	O Root of Jesse, you stand as a signal for the nations; kings fall silent before you whom the peoples acclaim. O come to deliver us, and do not delay.	Plant with flower, root with flowering stem
DECEMBER **20**	Isaiah 9:6; 22:22	**O Key of David**	O Key of David and Scepter of Israel, what you open no one else can close again; what you close no one can open. O come to lead the captive from prison; free those who sit in darkness and in the shadow of death.	Key
DECEMBER **21**	Isaiah 9:1; Psalm 19:6–7	**O Rising Dawn**	O Rising Dawn, you are the splendor of eternal light and the sun of justice. O come and enlighten those who sit in darkness and in the shadow of death.	Sun, sunrise
DECEMBER **22**	Isaiah 2:4; 9:5; Psalm 2:7–8; Ephesians 2:14–20	**O King of the Gentiles (Nations)**	O King whom all the peoples desire, you are the cornerstone which makes all one. O come and save us whom you made from clay.	Crown
DECEMBER **23**	Isaiah 7:14; 33:22	**O Emmanuel or O God with Us**	O Emmanuel, you are our king and judge, the One whom the peoples await and their Savior. O come and save us, Lord, our God.	Chalice and host, manger

18 THE **OUR FATHER**

Objective
To grow in understanding of the Our Father; to make a booklet that could often be used in prayer

Background for Catechists
As Christian Catholics today, we have many ways to pray. The *Catechism of the Catholic Church* tells us that the Lord's Prayer was given to us by Jesus as an example of how to pray. Through this prayer, we encounter a summary of the gospel message (nos. 2759–2776).

Some of the many "messages" in the Lord's Prayer:

- Jesus invites us not to simply pray to *his* Father, but to *ours*, for we are all daughters and sons of God.
- Likewise, we do not pray to *my* Father. There is no me, my, or I in this prayer. We are all one. God is our Father.
- The Our Father contains seven petitions. They teach us what we need to live happy, holy lives.
- The first three petitions help us to understand and grow closer to God; the last four teach us to ask for what we need, not just for ourselves but for the whole human family.

Materials
- ☐ Make pages for a booklet using the phrase from the Our Father, the short explanation and directions for that page on the bottom of each sheet (see the handout).
- ☐ Scissors
- ☐ Crayons, markers, paint, pencils
- ☐ Magazines and newspapers
- ☐ Colored paper

Lesson Starter
Ask: *What is your favorite prayer? When/how did you learn the Our Father? When do you—do we as a Catholic community—pray the Our Father?*

Talk with your learners about their experiences of praying the Our Father. Ask them what their favorite line is. Invite them to share what they think of when they pray that line, what they think that line means.

Activity
To help children/youth first learn the prayer—or to review it to help their understanding go deeper—invite them to make an Our Father booklet. The line from the Our Father, one description of its meaning, and something to do for each page is contained on the handout. The best way to do this would be space it out, giving ten to fifteen minutes to it each week (one page a week) rather than doing it all at once.

Prayer Together
Our Father, who art in heaven, hallowed be thy Name; thy kingdom come, thy will be done, on earth as it is in heaven. Give us this day our daily bread, and forgive us our trespasses, as we forgive those who trespass against us; and lead us not into temptation, but deliver us from evil. Amen.

Options
- Send the booklet home to be done as a family activity, suggesting that a page a week be done, giving special emphasis to that line in family prayer.
- The Our Father has been rewritten many times, not because it's not a perfect prayer, but because, in the rewriting, it often helps us to discover anew the meaning of the words. Invite your learners to write each line a little differently.

Our Father, who art in heaven

When we say "our" we mean everyone. Heaven is wherever God is.

Cut out pictures (from magazines and newspapers) of some of the many people who were created by God.

Hallowed be thy name

Hallowed means holy or sacred.

Using gold, silver, or brightly colored paper, cut out the word "God." Paste the letters on the page; decorate the page, showing how special God's name is.

Thy kingdom come

God's kingdom can be present here and now because of the way we act: caring for the needy, including everyone, and living in peace.

Draw a picture of yourself bringing love and peace by the way you act.

Thy will be done on earth as it is in heaven

We work for a time when all people will do what God wants: loving and caring for one another.

Paint a picture of people helping, caring, and loving one another.

Give us this day our daily bread

We pray for all that we need for each day.

Cut out magazine pictures of things we need each day to be alive, to live lives fully, to live safely and for others.

And forgive us our trespasses

God doesn't want us to harm or hurt people. When we do, we ask God to forgive us.

Draw a picture of something you want to say "I'm sorry" for.

As we forgive those who trespass against us

We are called to be like God. We forgive others when they hurt us.

Draw or write ways you can show forgiveness (for example, by giving a hug or saying "I forgive you").

And lead us not into temptation, but deliver us from evil

We ask God to help us make good choices and avoid temptation.

Draw two roads: on one print some temptations. On the other (a bigger road) print loving acts. Color brightly.

For thine is the kingdom, and the power, and the glory forever and ever

This ancient acclamation is sometimes added to Jesus' prayer.

Paint this page with bright colors and "fireworks," to show God's glory.

19 PATRON SAINTS

Objective

To reflect on a patron saint through a cinquain poem

Background for Catechists

Many early churches were built over the graves of martyrs and were named in honor of the martyr, expecting that she or he would be an intercessor for those who worshiped there. After some time, churches were dedicated to other saints who were not martyrs.

Our tradition encourages the giving of a saint's name at baptism, and seeing that saint as a model of discipleship and as an intercessor.

A third observance of patron saints is that most saints have been designated by the church to be patrons (benefactors/intercessors) for specific groups, activities, professions, causes, etc.

Materials

☐ Copies of the handout
☐ Books of patron saints
☐ Printouts from the Internet about various patron saints
☐ Pencils and paper

Lesson Starter

Ask: *Do you know someone (a family member, a friend, for example) whom you look up to, whom you go to for help, especially because of their expertise or interest in a particular subject—for example, for playing baseball or for being an artist? That's similar to patron saints in our Catholic family.*

Share with your learners the various ways we relate to patron saints: our names, parish names, and saints for various causes and interests. Talk about some of the saints who are the patron saints of your learners; explore with them some of the patron saints of various hobbies, life situations, and vocations.

Talk with them about the reality that giving attention to patron saints does not mean that we do not approach God directly; it is similar to asking a friend to pray for you, while you also pray. In this case, the friend is in heaven—this is an example of the communion of saints at work.

Activity

Invite your learners to learn more about one or two patron saints—theirs, their parish's, or others that they are interested in. Those listed on the handout can be a start.

As they learn about their saint(s), invite them to write a cinquain, capturing some of the essence of the saint's life. Write the following cinquain on the board and use it as an example to demonstrate the structure of the poem:

> Jesus
> Compassionate, Trustworthy
> Comforting, Forgiving, Challenging
> Taught us to be fully human
> Redeemer

Prayer Together

Saints of God
Holy, Faithful
Empowering, Providing, Loving
Witnesses

Options

- Learners can work individually or in small groups.
- Invite your learners to write a prayer to the saint they have chosen.
- Create a poster display of all the cinquains for your building hallway or church gathering space.
- Invite families to write a cinquain about their favorite saint.

Patron Saints

SOME OF OUR MANY PATRON SAINTS

Adopted children: St. Thomas More

Altar servers: St. John Berchmans

Animals: St. Francis of Assisi

Artists: St. Luke; Blessed Fra Angelico

Astronomers: St. Dominic

Boy Scouts: St. George

Carpenters: St. Joseph

Children: St. Nicholas

Computers: St. Isidore of Seville

Deacons: St. Stephen

Doctors: St. Luke

Dogs: St. Roch

Farmers: St. Isidore the Farmer

Firefighters: St. Florian

Fishermen: St. Andrew the Apostle

Grandparents: Sts. Anne and Joachim

Lost items: St. Anthony

Messengers: Gabriel the Archangel

Musicians: St. Cecilia

Safe journey: Raphael the Archangel

Students and scholars: St. Thomas Aquinas

Television: St. Clare of Assisi

Waiters/Waitresses: St. Martha

Directions for Writing a Cinquain

LINE ONE: A one word noun: a person, place, or thing

LINE TWO: Two adjectives that describe the person/place/thing

LINE THREE: Three "ing" words that describe the noun: what the person/place/thing does

LINE FOUR: A phrase or sentence about the person/place/thing

LINE FIVE: A synonym for the noun (another word for the person/place/thing; rename it)

PILGRIMAGES

Objective
To become aware of the practice of pilgrimage through participating in a prayerful pilgrimage

Background for Catechists
A pilgrimage is more than a trip; the journey itself represents our life journeys—with ourselves, with others, with life's ups and downs. Pilgrimages help us take time to experience God in new ways and to grow closer to God.

Materials
- ☐ The opening prayer might be on PowerPoint
- ☐ 3 x 5 cards with questions
- ☐ Copies of the handout for the ten children/youth for the closing prayer

Lesson Starter
Ask: *Have you ever taken a trip? What special place(s) have you visited? Why was it special?*

Talk about Christians embarking on special trips: pilgrimages, times to reflect on the constant presence of God, especially in places that shout to us of God's presence.

Activity
Invite your learners to go on a short pilgrimage.

Recall Mary's journeys: visit to Elizabeth, trip to Bethlehem, flight to Egypt, traveling to the temple, and following Jesus to Calvary.

Mary made interior journeys as well; from confusion (annunciation) to understanding; from worry (journey to the temple) to relief at finding Jesus; from sorrow (Calvary) to joy (Easter).

Divide your group into pairs as well as sides 1 and 2 for the opening prayer.

After the opening prayer, give each child a 3 x 5 card and ask them to answer the following:
- On your life journey, what are some gifts God has given you?
- What are some hard things that happen in your life journey? What has helped you to get through them?
- Tell about a time when you really felt God with you.

As you lead the pilgrimage (to a place the children/youth are yet unaware of), invite the pairs to walk together, sharing their thoughts about the questions.

Upon arriving at your destination (a prayer room, a shrine on the parish grounds, under trees, etc.), lead this threefold activity:
- Invite them to reflect on what they shared on the journey as you ask:
  - » *Did you discover anything new about yourself? about others because of your partner's thoughts? about God?*
- Remind them that a pilgrimage takes people to a holy place. Ask: *Is this a holy place?* Through discussion, help them realize that wherever this pilgrimage has taken them, it is a holy place. We believe that any place where two are three are gathered in Jesus' name is a holy place; all creation is holy and graced.
- Pray one decade of the Rosary based on one of the journeys of Mary, e.g., the visitation. Before each Hail Mary, have a different child focus the meditation (see handout).

Prayer Together
(This activity is a prayer and is intertwined with various ways of prayer.)

Option
Invite parents to join your group for this pilgrimage. Parents could form pairs among themselves or be paired with their child.

Opening Prayer before the Journey

LEADER: Let us pray.

SIDE 1: May the Lord watch over us and guide us on our journey— this pilgrimage and the journey of our lives.

SIDE 2: May no harm come to us, and may we reach our destination in peace and safety.

ALL: We ask this through Jesus, who said, "Follow me." Amen.

Prayers before each Hail Mary
(DURING THE CLOSING PRAYER)

1 Thank you, Lord, for the example of Mary, who journeyed to go to the aid of Elizabeth. Hail Mary...

2 Help us to be ready, like Mary, to give a helping hand when it is needed. Hail Mary...

3 Loving God, who asked Mary to bring Jesus to Elizabeth, use us to bring Jesus to the people we meet each day. Hail Mary...

4 Lord, help us to welcome you with joy. Help us to recognize you when you come into our lives. Hail Mary...

5 With Mary, we thank you, Gracious God, for sending your Son to become one of us. Hail Mary...

6 We praise you, Loving God, for your majesty and your mercy. Hail Mary...

7 We are sorry for not showing more clearly in our lives the joy of being Christians. Hail Mary...

8 We pray for mothers and fathers, that they may surround their children with joy and care, supported by the people around them. Hail Mary...

9 We thank you, Lord, for doing great things for ordinary people like us. Hail Mary...

10 We thank you, Gracious God, for always being with us on our journey. Hail Mary...

21 PRAYER, FASTING, ALMSGIVING

Objective
To delve into the practices of prayer, fasting, and almsgiving, especially as practices that permeate our entire lives

Background for Catechists
Three traditional practices are observed in Lent: prayer, fasting, almsgiving.

In reality, these practices are integral to our entire lives every day of the year. We concentrate upon them during Lent so that they might permeate our lives all year long.

The *United States Catholic Catechism for Adults* reminds us: "Definitions of prayer are important, but insufficient. There is a huge difference between knowing about prayer and praying. On this issue, the Rule of St. Benedict is clear, 'If a man wants to pray, let him go and pray.'"

Usually, fasting refers to restricting some type of food or drink. Since we do this to become more aware of God in our life, a question might be: "What's cluttering my life so that there isn't enough room for God—and others?" Almsgiving is closely tied to fasting: when we refrain from our usual meals and snacks, the money saved is given to others. Today's understanding of almsgiving goes beyond writing a check. There are multiple ways we can give of ourselves, all we have.

Materials
- ☐ Bibles
- ☐ Scripture concordance
- ☐ Copies of handout
- ☐ Large poster boards
- ☐ Tape
- ☐ Markers, crayons, pencils
- ☐ Parish bulletins, diocesan and local newspapers, articles and pictures from the Internet

Lesson Starter
Ask: *What are some things that followers of Jesus do?*

Use the handout to explain the practices of prayer, fasting, and almsgiving—Lenten practices that are also central to our life all year long.

Activity
Divide your group into smaller groups. Give each group one of the practices: prayer, fasting, or almsgiving. Depending upon the size of your group you may have one group, or more than one, for each practice.

Through discussion and research, invite each group to make a triptych about their practice (a set of three panels, hinged or folded so that the two wing panels fold over the large center one; this also makes it easy to stand). The three panels could include:
- Passages from Scripture about the practice
- Some possible ways they as young learners could live the practice
- Pictures and articles that illustrate people living the practice

Prayer Together
God, who calls us to discipleship, strengthen us in prayer, as we strive to always be one with you. Support us in our fasting, as we make more room for you. Guide us in our almsgiving, as we respond to the needs of all in your family, our sisters and brothers.

Options
The activity might be narrowed, concentrating on particular seasons of the year, since these three practices permeate our entire life as disciples. For instance: how might we pray, fast, and give alms during Advent? During the Easter season? During Ordinary Time?

Prayer, Fasting, and Almsgiving

	SOME SCRIPTURE QUOTES	MEANING	SOME EXAMPLES
Prayer	1 THESS 5:17 MT 6:9–13 1 COR 14:15	The many forms and methods of prayer that we have enable us to be more aware of our relationship with God, our unity with God, communicating with God, strengthening our unity with God, and reaching out to others.	Liturgy and sacraments, meditation, *Lectio Divina*, Liturgy of the Hours, the Rosary, litanies, Centering Prayer, family prayer, prayer before meals, silence.
Fasting	2 SAM 1:12 PS 35:13 JOEL 2:12–15 MT 6:16–18 LK 2:37 ACTS 9:9	To fast is to intentionally remove something from our lives, to empty ourselves so that we make space for God. Often, fasting is going without meat, a meal, or something we like to eat. It can also be anything that has become an excess or a detriment in our lives.	Fast from candy, complaining, arguing, TV and video games; eat simpler meals.
Almsgiving	TOB 4:7–11 MARK 12:43 LUKE 19:8–10 GAL 5:13 2 COR 9:6	The usual understanding of almsgiving—in all religious traditions—is any monetary help given to those who are in need.	Giving of money to help others, sharing of possessions, giving of my time and myself, caring for the earth.

22 SACRAMENTALITY

Objective

To become aware of the saramentality of life through intense watching and listening to the ordinary and everyday

Background for Catechists

Catholics believe—very strongly—in sacramentality, the principle that says everything in creation—people, movements, places, environment—can reveal God. Everything is sacred, because all comes from God. God is always present to us; we respond to God's grace through the ordinary and everydayness of our lives.

Saint Francis of Assisi tells this wonderful story: "I once spoke to my friend, an old squirrel, about the sacraments—he got so excited and ran into a hollow in his tree and came back holding some acorns, an owl feather, and a ribbon he found. And I just smiled and said, 'Yes, dear, you understand; everything imparts God's grace.'"

Materials

☐ Copies of handout
☐ Disposable cameras for those who don't have cameras or cell phones
☐ Poster boards
☐ Glue
☐ Pencils, crayons, markers

Lesson Starter

Say: *Have you ever had the experience—no matter where you looked—of seeing love (or kindness, or caring)? There are some things that seem to be everywhere—if we just look. That's one of the wonderful things about who we are as Catholics. We believe that everywhere we look, everything that we do, can reveal God's presence to us. We find God everywhere, in all things.*

Share with the learners the Catholic belief in sacramentality, including the story of St. Francis and the squirrel.

Activity

Invite the children/youth to go in search of sacramentality—signs of God's presence everywhere in their everyday world. Invite them to use their cameras or cell phones (or provide disposable cameras to those who need one). Ask them to "watch and listen" during the coming week and to take photos of places, things, events, and people that show God to them. Copy the handout and send it home with the children in order to explain the activity. Encourage them to make the "search for sacramentality" a family activity.

In a following week, invite the learners to arrange their pictures on their poster board (or in a PowerPoint), with a short phrase/sentence explaining why/how this was a sign of God's presence or of the holiness of life.

Prayer Together

In the snow and the sunshine, God of Beauty, we see you there. In the antics of kittens and puppies, God of Joy, we see you there. In time with friends and people who help us, God of Relationships, we see you there.

Options

■ Keep the posters in your learning space and/or highlight one each week, incorporating the thoughts into opening or closing prayer for your session.
■ Display the pictures in the hallways and/or gathering space of church.

Dear Parents,

Today in our faith formation session, we explored the Catholic belief of sacramentality: the conviction that our God is ever present—we see and meet God all the time through the ordinary and everyday: other people, things, events, and places.

Because God became human, God is seen, touched, and heard in our human living. We live in a sacred world that was created by God. Therefore, all of creation—from our natural environment to human people and the happenings of everyday life—gives us the opportunity to glimpse and experience God's presence.

So many ordinary and everyday happenings and things give us a glimpse of what God is really like. In our visible world of sights, sounds, and encounters we see and experience the invisible God.

As we reflect on this powerful reality of sacramentality, your child has been invited to be especially on the lookout this week: to "watch and listen" for places, things, events, and people who reveal God to her/him—and then to take a photo of it.

We invite your family to join in this search. At your evening meal, or at bedtime, invite each family member to talk about something that reminded them of God that day: a person, some happening, an object, a place, etc.

Encourage your child, too, to take the camera everywhere with her/him, spending this week in a prayerful watching and listening stance. As we see and hear, we learn more about God and we experience God in our everyday life.

Enjoy! May this week deepen your awareness of God with you and of your love and caring for each other.

In an awareness of God's presence with each of us,

SACRAMENTALS

Objective

To become more deeply aware of the sacramentals of the church in our daily lives

Background for Catechists

Vatican II's *Constitution on the Sacred Liturgy* (no. 60) states that sacramentals are "sacred signs which bear a resemblance to the sacraments." They help people "to receive the chief effects of the sacraments, and various occasions in life are rendered holy." Sacramentals underscore the conviction that all creation holds potential for recognizing God's presence and blessing.

Sacramentals can be prayers (Sign of the Cross, novenas, Stations), objects (medals, statues, vestments, oil, rosaries, holy water, ashes, blessed palms, crucifixes, crosses, icons, incense, the altar, Advent wreath, candles, Paschal Candle, baptismal candle, sanctuary lamp), actions (genuflection, bowing, folding hands, fasting), and religious ceremonies/rites (laying on of hands, pilgrimages, blessings).

Materials

- [ ] Handout
- [ ] Pencils
- [ ] You might place some sacramentals in places where you will go/pass on your walk and/or arrange for people (some parishioners) to be in some of the places: genuflecting, making the sign of the cross, hands folded, etc.).

Lesson Starter

Say: *Do you have anything with you today that reminds you of your family, or one of your friends? These things are not your family or your friends, but they point to and bring to your mind (and heart) your friends or family. The church has things (and actions, prayers,*

and rituals) like that too. When we use them, pray them, or do them, they remind us of God's presence and grace at work in us. They help us to keep our minds (and hearts) connected to and focused on God's love and our faith in God.

Share with your learners some of the sacramentals of the church, explaining those with which they might not be familiar.

Activity

Say: *Let's go on a treasure hunt. I'm going to lead; as we walk, look for some of the sacramentals that are listed on your handout. When you see one, jot down on your handout where you saw it.*

You might want to ask some parents to go on this walk, so that each adult has four or five children/youth to guide. Map out your walk ahead of time and give the adult helpers all the information of where to go. Each group can travel the journey at its own speed and in whichever order the leader desires.

When everyone reassembles after the walk, share what was discovered. How many sacramentals were found by the whole group (rather than individually)?

Prayer Together

God of all things, you surround us with many signs of your presence. Teach us to cherish and reverently use the sacramentals of our faith: in our prayer, in our actions, in our service as our love for you grows and spreads to others.

Option

The children/youth could be given the handout to use on their own for the next two weeks. Every time they encounter a sacramental, they write where and when they saw it or used it.

The Gift of Sacramentals

As we go on our treasure hunt, look for some of the sacramentals we've talked about. When you see one, write down what it is, and where you saw it.

Sacramental

_____
_____
_____

Sacramental

_____
_____
_____

Sacramental

_____
_____
_____

Sacramental

_____
_____
_____

Sacramental

_____
_____
_____

Sacramental

_____
_____
_____

Sacramentals you MIGHT see:

Sign of the cross, novenas, Stations of the Cross, medals, statues, vestments, oil, rosaries, holy water, ashes, blessed palms, crucifixes, crosses, icons, incense, the altar, Advent wreath, candles, Paschal Candle, baptismal candle, sanctuary lamp, genuflection, bowing, folding hands, laying on of hands, and blessings.

24 SACRAMENTS

Objective

Using everyday objects to discover new ways of appreciating the sacraments

Background for Catechists

We are a sacramental people; our lives are grounded in celebrating the sacraments. Because we are people who touch, see, hear, smell, and taste, the church uses familiar objects and actions to help us experience the sacraments in our lives.

Materials

- ☐ Pictures of everyday signs/symbols, such as a wedding ring, American flag, stop sign
- ☐ A table with symbols/signs (or pictures) used in the sacraments: water, oil, light, fire, bread, white garment
- ☐ A second table with everyday objects, such as a toy car, key, funnel, magnifying glass, book, box of crayons, candy bar
- ☐ Copies of handout; pencils or pens

Lesson Starter

Say: *What are some things in our lives that are signs/symbols? When we see them, we know what they mean—usually without words.*

Write the names of the seven sacraments on the board. Show some everyday signs and symbols. Invite a discussion of what is behind each sign/symbol. Is a wedding ring just a piece of jewelry or does it tell us something more? Using the symbols/signs on the sacraments table, invite the children/youth to recall the reality to which that symbol/sign points. For example:

- Water, necessary for life, is used in baptism when we are immersed in new life with Jesus.
- Oil is a sign of healing and strength. In some cultures, oil is used to bless royalty. Oil is used in several sacraments as a

sign of God's healing and strength and God's choice of us as Jesus' disciples.

Activity

Often, everyday objects help us explore the "mystery" in important things in our lives.

- Distribute the handout.
- Invite them to choose three sacraments.
- Have them choose an object (the second table) that tells them something about the sacrament. This isn't a symbol/ sign to use in the sacrament, but an opportunity to use their imaginations to see how that object helps them understand the sacrament in a new way.
- What is the object like; what are some of its characteristics? What does this say about the sacrament? For example, the sacrament of reconciliation is like a magnifying glass because it helps us to see our lives in bigger ways, through God's eyes.
- Invite each learner to fill in the lines on the handout.
- Take time for discussion, especially comparing the ideas that came from different objects used for the same sacrament.

Prayer Together

God of Signs and Symbols, the sacraments reveal your love and your call to us to be disciples of Jesus. Surprise us with new understandings. Deepen in us new appreciations. Challenge us to new ways of living as your sacramental people.

Option

Take your learners to a nearby dollar store, giving each $1.00 (plus tax, if necessary). Invite them to purchase one object to use as a symbol to describe one of the sacraments.

Signs of the Sacraments

Fill in the lines to describe what the symbols
you chose tell about the sacrament.

The sacrament of _____

is like a _____

because _____.

The sacrament of _____

is like a _____

because _____.

The sacrament of _____

is like a _____

because _____.

Objective

To discern and discover some facts about a few of our saints

Background for Catechists

The saints have an important role in Catholic life. The long list of saints in our tradition includes all kinds of people: married couples, farmers, students, young people, priests and religious, actors, teachers, artists, and many more. The most important reality about them, however, is their deep relationship with God and their service to God's people.

Materials

☐ Learners' texts: lessons on various saints

☐ Several books on lives of the saints

☐ Paper and pencils

☐ Copies of handout

Lesson Starter

Say: *Do you enjoy hearing stories about your parents and your grandparents? Because they are members of our families, we want to know everything we can, and we love to hear the funny stories, the important stories, the small stories, and the big ones. Because saints are part of our Catholic family, it is important for us to know as much as we can about them—how they lived, what characteristics people remember about them, and in which ways they developed their relationship with God.*

Activity

Explain that many years ago, there was a television show called *To Tell the Truth*. (Some episodes are on YouTube.) Three people all claimed to be a certain person. The host told that person's story (which was funny, serious, inspirational, having to do with their profession or the cause they were involved in). Four celebrity panelists questioned the contestants (addressing them as Number 1, Number 2, and Number 3) to determine which was actually the person he or she claimed to be, and who were the imposters. After the four panelists questioned the three, the panelists voted separately about who they thought was the real person associated with the story.

Divide your learners into groups of three, giving each group the name of a saint (e.g., St. Peter, St. Francis of Assisi, St. Catherine of Siena, St. Thérèse, or a saint studied during the year). Invite each group to write a possible script for a "To Tell the Truth" episode featuring their saint. (The beginning of a sample is in the handout.)

When the groups have finished, each takes a turn presenting their episode to the others. The three in the group can take the role of those claiming to be the saint. Four people from your whole group can be chosen to be the panelists asking the questions. They will need only the questions to ask; the three "saints/claiming to be saints" will have the answers.

Prayer Together

God of the Holy Ones, in every time and place there have been holy people who have modeled for us compassion, forgiveness, and giving themselves to others. May their witness encourage, support, and call us to be your faith-filled people.

Options

■ Every group could be given the same saint. It will be interesting to see the variety of questions.

■ Have the children/youth present their episodes for other grade levels or for their parents.

To Tell the Truth

ANNOUNCER: Number 1, what is your name, please?

NUMBER 1: My name is St. Paul.

ANNOUNCER: Number 2, what is your name, please?

NUMBER 2: My name is St. Paul.

ANNOUNCER: Number 3, what is your name, please?

NUMBER 3: My name is St. Paul.

ANNOUNCER: *(asks the audience to listen to the following affidavit)* Also known as Saul, I am St. Paul the Apostle, not one of the Twelve Apostles. After a conversion experience, I faithfully taught the gospel of Christ to the first-century world and founded several churches in Asia Minor and Europe.

1ST PANELIST: Why did God change your name from Saul to Paul?

NUMBER 1: God thought it sounded better; it sounded more Catholic.

NUMBER 2: He didn't. I used both names all the time.

NUMBER 3: It shows that there was a drastic change in my life.

2ND PANELIST: In your conversion experience, were you knocked off a horse?

NUMBER 1: It was actually a donkey.

NUMBER 2: No; there's no mention of a horse in the scriptural accounts.

NUMBER 3: Definitely. Look at the many pictures that have been painted throughout history.

3RD PANELIST: What is your favorite title for yourself?

NUMBER 1: The Thirteenth Apostle.

NUMBER 2: Apostle to the Gentiles.

NUMBER 3: The Traveling Apostle.

4TH PANELIST: If you were here today, how would you communicate and pass on Jesus' message?

NUMBER 1: Movies and TV.

NUMBER 2: I'm partial to letters.

NUMBER 3: Facebook and Twitter.

1ST PANELIST: What was your favorite city/town?

NUMBER 1: Rome, where I was born.

NUMBER 2: Damascus, where I was baptized.

NUMBER 3: Corinth; I wrote five letters to the Corinthians.

2ND PANELIST: In addition to your letters, how else could we find out about your life?

NUMBER 1: My autobiography.

NUMBER 2: The Acts of the Apostles.

NUMBER 3: There's a new TV show about me.

SCRIPTURE

Objective

To review, through a game, some of the key people, happenings, and themes contained in Scripture

Background for Catechists

Scripture is foundational to who we are as Catholics. A collection of books written by different people over a long period of time, Scripture is about God and God's relationship with us. The Bible teaches us how to live our lives, comforts us in times of need, challenges us, and helps us to know who God is, how we are loved, and all that we are called to be and do.

Psalm 119:105 tells us the importance of Scripture for us: "Your word is a lamp to my feet and a light to my path."

Materials

☐ A box with 26 slips of paper, each containing a letter of the alphabet
☐ Paper, pencils
☐ Bibles
☐ Copies of handout

Lesson Starter

Say: *What do you like to read the most: poetry, stories about important people, history? We— as God's people—have a book (many books within a book) that is filled with many kinds of writings: laws, history, wisdom sayings and proverbs, poetry, songs, prayers, gospels, parables, letters, prophecy, and apocalyptic literature. The Bible is a library of books. The authors were inspired by the Holy Spirit in their writing. It also has the human touch from its authors. Paul is different from David, who is different from James or Moses.*

The Bible is divided into two main sections:

- *The Old Testament tells about God's relationship with humanity before the birth of Jesus.*

- *The New Testament describes the teachings and life of Jesus and the early church.*

Use the list on the handout to review or acquaint your learners with some of the books of the Bible. Have them locate them in their Bibles.

Activity

Scripture Scattergories is a game to review and remember the people, themes, and events of Scripture.

Divide your learners into small teams (three or four to a team).

For each round, invite a child/youth to take from the alphabet box one of the slips of paper.

Each team then comes up with, and explains, three Scripture-related words (a person, a theme in Scripture, an event, happening, or object) that begins with the letter on the drawn slip.

Prayer Together

Come, Holy Spirit. In God's word help us to hear your voice. Deepen our wisdom to understand God's message. Give us strength to follow God's call.

Options

- In deciding their three words, the teams also could use alliteration, for example: Challenging Covenant, Meticulous Martha, Prayerful Psalms.
- When the teams decide on their three words, they draw a picture/symbol of each. The others need to guess what their words are.
- Within a specified time, each team works together to come up with as many words (instead of just the three)— for the given letter—as they can. In reporting back, they give the words and a short explanation for each.

Old Testament Books

The Pentateuch
Genesis
Exodus
Leviticus
Numbers
Deuteronomy

Historical Books
Joshua
Judges
Ruth
1 Samuel
2 Samuel
1 Kings
2 Kings
1 Chronicles
2 Chronicles
Ezra
Nehemiah
Tobit
Judith
Esther
1 Maccabees
2 Maccabees

Wisdom and Poetry Books
Job
Psalms
Proverbs
Ecclesiastes
Song of Songs
Wisdom
Sirach

The Prophets
Isaiah
Jeremiah
Lamentations
Baruch
Ezekiel
Daniel
Hosea
Joel
Amos
Obadiah
Jonah
Micah
Nahum
Habakkuk
Zephaniah
Haggai
Zechariah
Malachi

New Testament Books

Matthew
Mark
Luke
John

Acts of
the Apostles

Romans
1 Corinthians
2 Corinthians
Galatians
Ephesians
Philippians
Colossians
1 Thessalonians

2 Thessalonians
1 Timothy
2 Timothy
Titus
Philemon
Hebrews
James
1 Peter
2 Peter
1 John
2 John
3 John
Jude

Revelation

STATIONS OF THE CROSS

Objective

To review the Stations of the Cross and explore how they are experienced in our lives and in the world around us

Background for Catechists

The Stations of the Cross (also called the Way of the Cross, *Via Crucis*, and *Via Dolorosa*) is a devotion that commemorates the death of Jesus. Each of the fourteen stations represents an event during Jesus' passion and death at Calvary on Good Friday. The devotion consists of prayers and meditations on these fourteen critical events from Scripture or tradition.

Originally done only outdoors, the Stations were allowed inside churches in the mid-eighteenth century. Eventually fixed at fourteen, the Stations became a familiar feature in Catholic churches.

Materials

☐ Textbooks: lessons on the Stations
☐ Booklets of Stations of the Cross
☐ Paper
☐ Newspapers, magazines, Internet access
☐ Crayons, markers, paint

Lesson Starter

Ask: *Do you—or anyone you know—keep a scrapbook of important events? Since the final events of Jesus' life on earth are very important, a reflective prayer on these events—often with pictures/statues—is celebrated in the church. It is like a scrapbook of this part of Jesus' life: the Stations of the Cross.*

Use the handout to teach or review with your learners the fourteen events of Jesus' last days depicted in the Stations. Tell the children that often—in addition to reflecting on the episodes in Jesus' life—people also think about how the stations are happening today: in their own personal lives and in the lives of others in our world (especially the needy and the suffering).

Activity

Give each child/youth one of the stations, or form groups if you have more than fourteen learners. (Two children could also work on two stations together.)

Invite them to draw/paint pictures and/or find pictures or news stories of how their station might be happening in their personal lives as well as in the lives of others throughout the world.

Pass out the handout. The handout might provide them some beginning reflections, but they do not need to be restricted by this, since there are many possibilities.

Prayer Together

Jesus, our brother, you suffered and died because of how you lived. You would not stop living unconditional love. Sometimes, as your followers, we go through difficult things. Teach us to love totally. Often in our world today, people suffer and are mistreated; teach us how to reach out in compassion.

Options

- Invite the children/youth to find music (religious and/or contemporary) that coincides with the modern-day meanings of the Stations.
- Invite them to write prayers for themselves and for those who are suffering.
- If there is another person in the Station (about Jesus' life), invite the children/youth to complete the sentence: If I had been _____.

Stations of the Cross in our lives, in the life of the world

STATION 1: Jesus is condemned to death

- Has anyone ever said things about me that were not true?
- Are there people in our world who are judged unfairly?

STATION 2: Jesus carries the cross

- What cross have I carried?
- Who are the people in the world who are carrying heavy crosses?

STATION 3: Jesus falls the first time

- When have I been hurt and not wanted to continue?
- Who in our world seem to be without hope?

STATION 4: Jesus meets his mother

- When have I brought comfort to someone?
- Who is suffering in the world?

STATION 5: Simon helps Jesus carry the cross

- Have I ever helped someone who was having a hard time?
- Who in our world needs our help?

STATION 6: Veronica Wipes Jesus' face

- Have I ever done something that helped someone feel better?
- Who in our world needs small acts of kindness?

STATION 7: Jesus falls the second time

- Have I ever had someone push me down?
- Are there people in our world who are mocked because they keep falling?

STATION 8: Jesus meets women who are crying

- Is there something that makes me sad?
- Who in our world are hurting and need comfort?

STATION 9: Jesus falls a third time

- When do I get discouraged?
- Who are some people in our world who are discouraged, maybe all the time?

STATION 10: Jesus is stripped of his clothes

- Are there things I need to give up?
- Are there people who have been stripped of who they are because of illness or poverty or violence?

STATION 11: Jesus is nailed to the cross

- Have I ever forgiven someone who has hurt me?
- Are there places in our world where people don't forgive, where people are kept "nailed down"?

STATION 12: Jesus dies on the cross

- Am I afraid of being crucified because I'm a Christian?
- Who/where/when in our world are people willing to love—no matter what the cost?

STATION 13: Jesus is taken down from the cross

- What do I do for a friend?
- Who in our world helps people in crisis, in need?

STATION 14: Jesus is buried

- Have I ever thought something was over, only to discover a new beginning?
- What people in our world need a new beginning?

THE **DAYS** OF **HOLY WEEK**

Objective

To delve deeper into the meaning of the days of Holy Week, suggesting ways of praying and living the days

Background for Catechists

One definition of "holy" is "set apart." Christians set apart an entire week, the last week of Lent, to remember the final days of Christ's life, especially his suffering, death, burial, and resurrection.

The last days of Holy Week are called the Triduum. The liturgical services of these days—Holy Thursday through the Easter Vigil—are viewed as one continuing celebration, rather than separate events.

It is believed that Holy Week probably developed in fourth-century Jerusalem. Christians from all over the world took pilgrimages to the Holy Land; the church of Jerusalem provided for them prayer times dedicated to reenacting the final events of Christ's life.

Materials

☐ Copies of handout
☐ Poster board and/or paper
☐ Bibles
☐ Pencils, crayons, markers, paint

Lesson Starter

Say: *Have you ever celebrated something special for longer than one day? Within our church family we do that. One of the times we do it is during a special time named Holy Week.*

Share the meaning and timing of Holy Week and something about each day of the week (using the handout as a starter). Invite them to share what they remember from their celebrations of Holy Week in the past few years, with their families and with the parish. What do they remember seeing and doing? How did they pray?

Activity

- Establish four small groups (the number of topics to be learned)
- Assign a different topic to each group: Palm Sunday, Holy Thursday, Good Friday, Holy Saturday.
- Invite the children/youth to work together to do all or some of these activities (they might create a large poster or do them on individual pages to assemble into a group book):
  » Identify the Scripture passages that recount the day
  » Draw/paint a picture of the day in Jesus' life
  » Draw/paint a picture of how the church celebrates the day today
  » Write a prayer that might be prayed on this day
  » Suggest some activities that families might do on the day

Prayer Together

Father of Unconditional Love, we remember the last events of the life of Jesus, which led to his suffering and death. Deepen in us Jesus' life: his faithfulness, his trust in you, his care for others. Help us to die to ourselves, rising to a life of love and joy.

Options

- Display the posters in the gathering space of church to be shared with the parish.
- Collate, copy, and send home the prayers and suggestions.

The Major Liturgies of Holy Week

PALM SUNDAY

- Holy Week begins with the sixth Sunday in Lent. This Sunday observes the triumphal entry of Jesus into Jerusalem that was marked by the crowds, who were in Jerusalem for Passover, waving palm branches and proclaiming him as the king.

- This Sunday is also known as Passion Sunday to commemorate the beginning of Holy Week and Jesus' final journey to the cross.

HOLY THURSDAY

- Holy Thursday is more than just the lead-in to Good Friday; it is, in fact, the oldest of the celebrations of Holy Week.

- Holy Thursday commemorates Jesus eating the Passover meal with his apostles, giving the church the gift of the Eucharist.

- The gospel used in the Holy Thursday liturgy comes from John's gospel: Jesus washing the feet of the apostles.

- On Holy Thursday (or another day in Holy Week), there is a liturgy in cathedral churches, attended by priests and/or representatives from each parish. At this "Chrism Mass" the bishop blesses the chrism used for baptism, confirmation, holy orders; the oil of the sick for the sacrament of the sick; and the oil of catechumens.

GOOD FRIDAY

- On this day, the church commemorates Jesus' arrest, trial, crucifixion and suffering, death, and burial.

- The Good Friday services are often celebrated around 3:00 PM, to correspond to the final words of Jesus from the cross (Matthew 27:46–50).

- The Good Friday service includes four parts: 1) Liturgy of the Word— reading of the Passion, 2) Intercessory prayers for the church and the entire world, Christians and non-Christians, 3)Veneration of the Cross, and 4) Communion.

HOLY SATURDAY

- On Holy Saturday, the church waits; the altar is left bare, and liturgy is not celebrated until the Easter Vigil, after dark.

- The Easter Vigil service, which begins the liturgies of Easter Sunday, is divided into four parts: 1) Service of Light, 2) Liturgy of the Word, 3) Liturgy of Baptism, and 4) Liturgy of the Eucharist.

- The Paschal, or Easter, candle, blessed during the Service of Light, symbolizes Jesus Christ's rising as the light of the world. The candle is used throughout the next year for baptisms and funerals.

THE **LITURGICAL YEAR**

Objective
To discover more about the church's liturgical year (through a creative design)

Background for Catechists
Thinking about a year, we might think of the calendar year or the school year. As a church, we have a year, too—the liturgical year, which marks the celebration of our liturgies and celebrates God's time. It is both eternal and timeless. In the liturgical year we remember the past, celebrate the present, and look to the future.

The liturgical year does not mark the passage of time, but celebrates more fully the mystery of Jesus Christ, from his birth until his ascension, the day of Pentecost, and his return in glory. During one year, the paschal mystery—the life, passion, death, resurrection, and ascension of Jesus—is viewed from different angles, in different lights.

The seasons of the liturgical year are: Advent, Christmas-Epiphany, Ordinary Time (broken into two parts), Lent, Triduum, Easter.

Materials
☐ Copies of handout
☐ Paper
☐ Pencils, crayons, markers

Lesson Starter
Ask: ***When does the new year begin? Do we have different types of "years"?*** (calendar year, fiscal year, school year, etc.)

Lead your learners in understanding the reason for, and the structure of, the liturgical year and an understanding of each season (handout).

Activity
Divide your group into six groups: Advent, Christmas-Epiphany, Ordinary Time, Lent, Triduum, Easter.

Using the handout and their memories of the various seasons, invite each group to design the cover/front page of their parish bulletin, telling about their season. Encourage them to use color and pictures as well as various "articles," including "news" articles, interviews, letters to the editor, Scripture passages and reflections, and suggestions of things to do.

Prayer Together
God of all Seasons, during our liturgical year we celebrate the life, death, and resurrection of your Son, Jesus. His life, teachings, and witness call us to live for every season: seasons of difficulties and joy, of worries and wonders, of compassion and caring, of peace-making and service. As we celebrate the mysteries of Jesus, deepen in us his life and your grace, so that we will be disciples in all seasons.

Options
- Talk with your bulletin editor, offering the designs for each liturgical season.
- As each liturgical season occurs, post the "front page" for that season in a special display in the church gathering space.
- Invite the groups to make a large poster (or PowerPoint or movie) about their liturgical season.

The Liturgical Year

SEASON	TIME	MEANING	PRACTICES-RITUALS	SYMBOLS	SOME FEASTS	COLOR
ADVENT	*Four weeks preceding Christmas*	Joyful waiting for Jesus, who has already come	Advent wreath, Jesse Tree, Advent calendar, O Antiphons	Advent wreath	St. Nicholas, Immaculate Conception, Our Lady of Guadalupe	Purple
CHRISTMAS	*Christmas Eve to feast of Jesus' baptism*	Celebration of the birth of Jesus, of God becoming human	Blessing of the tree, 12 days of Christmas	Manger, light, gifts of magi	Holy Family, Solemnity of Mary, Epiphany	White
ORDINARY TIME	*Monday after feast of Jesus' baptism to Ash Wednesday*	Recalling the beginning of Jesus' public life	Focuses on primacy of Sunday; living Sunday well	Chi-Ro; the color green	Octave of Christian Unity	Green
LENT	*Ash Wednesday to Holy Thursday afternoon*	Conversion; Preparing for renewal of baptismal promises	Prayer, Fasting, and Almsgiving; Lenten resolutions	Cross, ashes, palms, nails, desert	St. Joseph	Purple
TRIDUUM	*Last three days of Holy Week*	Commemoration of Jesus' "passing over" from suffering-death to resurrection	Chrism Mass, blessing of oils, blessing of food	Bread-Wine, washing of feet, cross	Holy Thursday, Good Friday Easter Vigil	Thurs: White; Fri: Red Vigil: White
EASTER	*Easter Vigil through Pentecost Sunday*	Celebration of Resurrection, Ascension, and Pentecost; the fulfillment of Jesus' promise of the Holy Spirit	Renewal of baptismal promises, First Communions and confirmation; awareness of new life	Lily, Risen Christ, Paschal Candle, water	50 days of Easter, Ascension, Pentecost	White
ORDINARY TIME	*Monday after Pentecost to First Sunday of Advent*	Focusing on Jesus' life and teachings	Reminds us of the holiness of ordinary life; gratitude for God's presence in the everyday	Chi-Ro; the color green	Trinity Sunday, Feast of Corpus Christi, All Saints, All Souls, Christ the King	Green

30 THE **MYSTERIES** OF THE **ROSARY**

Objective
To become more aware of the names (and meanings) of the mysteries of the Rosary

Background for Catechists
A scriptural prayer, the Rosary reflects on key events in the life of Jesus and Mary. The Rosary is divided into five decades (or sections), each reflecting on a different event. These five events are grouped into a set of mysteries. For centuries, the church used three sets of mysteries. In 2002, Pope John Paul II proposed a fourth set: the Mysteries of Light or Luminous Mysteries.

The church suggests that these four sets be prayed on the following days:
- Joyful Mysteries: Monday and Saturday
- Sorrowful Mysteries: Tuesday and Friday
- Glorious Mysteries: Wednesday and Sunday
- Luminous Mysteries: Thursday

Materials
- ☐ Copies of handout
- ☐ Pencils
- ☐ Buttons
- ☐ The 25 names for the bingo squares are written on paper and placed in a box/basket.
- ☐ Rosary for each child, preferably different kinds, different colors

Lesson Starter
Say: *Do you like looking at photos of your family, or your friends? In many ways, we look at some of the photos, some of the life events, of Jesus and Mary, as we pray the Rosary.*

Explain that the Rosary is a meditation prayer. In addition to the prayers (the Hail Mary, the Our Father, the Apostles' Creed), each decade invites us to meditate, to think about one of the life events of Jesus and/or Mary.

Explain to the learners the four groups of mysteries and the events contained in each set.

Activity
Each person makes a bingo card by writing the mysteries, the titles of each group of mysteries, and "Hail Mary" in whichever order they would like on their card.

To play: the catechist chooses one slip from the box, naming what is written. Each learner places a button where that name is written on their card.

As children complete an entire row on their cards, either vertically or horizontally, they have a bingo and can choose a rosary for themselves. Continue playing until everyone bingos and chooses a rosary.

Prayer Together
Hail Holy Queen, Mother of mercy, our life, our sweetness, and our hope. To thee do we cry, poor banished children of Eve. To thee do we send up our sighs, mourning and weeping in this valley of tears. Turn then, most gracious advocate, thine eyes of mercy towards us. And after this, our exile, show unto us the blessed fruit of thy womb, Jesus. O clement, O loving, O sweet Virgin Mary.

Leader: *Pray for us, O holy mother of God.*

All: *That we may be made worthy of the promises of Christ.*

Options
- Instead of calling the mystery's name, a picture of the mystery is held up. Learners then place their marker on the name of the mystery on their card.
- Instead of using pictures or naming the mystery, the catechist might describe it. The learners find the correct name for the description given.

Rosary Bingo Card

<table>
<tr><td></td><td></td><td></td><td></td><td></td></tr>
<tr><td></td><td></td><td></td><td></td><td></td></tr>
<tr><td></td><td></td><td></td><td></td><td></td></tr>
<tr><td></td><td></td><td></td><td></td><td></td></tr>
<tr><td></td><td></td><td></td><td></td><td></td></tr>
</table>

THE MYSTERIES OF THE ROSARY

The Annunciation

The Visitation

The Nativity

The Presentation

The Finding of Jesus
in the Temple

The Baptism of Jesus

The Wedding at Cana

Proclamation
of the Kingdom

The Transfiguration

Institution of the Eucharist

The Agony in the Garden

The Scourging at the Pillar

The Crowning with Thorns

The Carrying of the Cross

The Crucifixion

The Resurrection

The Ascension

The Descent
of the Holy Spirit

The Assumption
of the Blessed Virgin

The Coronation
of the Blessed Virgin

TITLES OF THE MYSTERIES AND PRAYER TO ADD TO THE BINGO CARD

Joyful Mysteries

Sorrowful Mysteries

Glorious Mysteries

Luminous Mysteries

Hail Mary

31 THE **VIRTUES**

Objective

To discover ways to live the virtues in our everyday lives

Background for Catechists

Virtues are like habits; they need to be practiced for them to be alive, active, and a part of our lives. At baptism, we were given the three theological virtues: faith, hope, and charity (love). They are theological (study of God) because they come to us from God and lead us to deepen our relationship with God.

The four cardinal virtues (justice, prudence, temperance, and fortitude) come because we are human; we acquire them and they grow in us through education and good actions. The word *cardinal* comes from the Latin word for "hinge," which means that other virtues depend upon them. For example, when the virtue of temperance grows in us, it is also easier to develop virtues such as patience and living a healthy lifestyle. As these four virtues are developed in our lives, we become people of moral character, which means choosing to do the right thing, even if and when it might be difficult.

Materials

- ☐ Lessons from textbooks on the virtues
- ☐ Books from your parish library on the virtues (written for children/youth)
- ☐ Copies of the handout
- ☐ Paper, markers
- ☐ Flip cameras and/or PowerPoint

Lesson Starter

Ask: *Did you ever have an experience when you felt energy within yourself to help you do something that perhaps you thought you couldn't do?*

Explain that this is probably very true, since we have some gifts/habits because we are hu-man and some that have been especially given to us by God at baptism: the virtues. Distribute the handout and use it to explain the theological and cardinal virtues.

Explain these seven gifts/characteristics and explore times when they are operative in our lives. Remind the children/youth that these virtues are habits; the more we use them, the stronger they will be, and the stronger and more loving we will be in all our actions.

Activity

Divide your learners into seven groups of two (or three or four, depending upon your numbers). Give each group one of the virtues and invite them to design a commercial or an advertisement for their virtue. Encourage their creativity:

- ■ What is this virtue like?
- ■ Why is it important to have and develop?
- ■ What are some times and ways that it can be used?
- ■ What does it cost?

Gather the group together and invite them to share the results of their work.

Prayer Together

God of all good gifts, in baptism, you gave us gifts, three virtues, to grow closer to you. Help us to deepen these virtues of faith, hope, and love, as well as the virtues of prudence, justice, fortitude, and temperance, in all that we do.

Options

- ■ Post and/or share the commercials and advertisements throughout your building.
- ■ Ask local businesses if they would post the ads in their windows

The Theological Virtues

Faith is a gift as well as a response. God invites us to believe in him, to have a relationship with him. When we accept and respond enthusiastically to the invitation, every part of our life is affected by faith. We believe, and we live our faith anywhere and everywhere.

Hope is the trust that God will always be with us. Because of hope, we trust that God is with us through all things now, even difficult things, and God helps us live in a way that will keep us with him forever.

Charity/love is the foundation of the commandment to love God above all things, and our neighbor as ourselves. Love is more than a feeling; it is an attitude that expresses itself in our decisions and actions.

The Cardinal Virtues

Prudence helps us to stop and think before we act. It's the ability to know and judge whether to say something or do nothing at all. With this virtue we are able to see and understand what the right thing to do is in each circumstance.

Justice is the desire and the action to give to each person what is their due; it helps us treat each and every person rightly. Justice involves always thinking of the needs of others as much as our own.

Temperance is all about balance in our lives. It is the good habit that allows a person to relax, to enjoy life, to have fun without crossing the line, without going overboard. Too much play isn't good, but neither is all work and no play. Good food is important, but too much food harms our bodies, and too little likewise causes problems.

Fortitude is also called courage; it gives us the strength to not give up. Because of fortitude, we can act as a disciple of Jesus even when situations are difficult or there are obstacles in our way. It is the courage to do the right thing no matter what the cost.

WATER – HOLY WATER

Objective
To learn about holy water, one of our sacramentals; to write family blessing prayers

Background for Catechists
Throughout the history of God's people, we often encounter water, including the creation of the world, Noah and the flood, Moses and the Red Sea, John the Baptist baptizing with water, Jesus speaking about living water, and Jesus washing the feet of his disciples.

In our faith, water is used often: baptism, sprinkling at the beginning of Mass (the *asperges*), at the doors of the church, in various rites of blessing, at home for the blessing of persons and things, for the washing of the priest's hands during liturgy, and for the washing of feet on Holy Thursday. Water is also mingled with wine prior to the consecration at Mass.

Many churches today place their baptismal font at the entrance of the church as a reminder of the centrality of baptism in our faith lives.

Materials
- ☐ Bowls of water—one for every two or three children/youth
- ☐ Copies of handout
- ☐ Samples of blessing prayers
- ☐ Paper, pens or pencils
- ☐ Assembled booklets for each child
- ☐ Small bottles of holy water

Lesson Starter
Invite your learners to dip their fingers in the water. Invite them to take a moment to just feel it. Ask them to think of all the ways water is used—in their lives and in the life of the world.

Water is often used in the rites and celebrations of our faith. Invite them to name some. Talk with them about the meaning of each, reminding them of some they might not have

mentioned.

Share with them that holy water is used often in various blessing rites within the church and within the home.

Activity
Use the handout to help your learners think of family times and occasions and reasons when family members might bless each other.

Distribute paper and pens. Invite each child/youth to choose one occasion/reason from the list, and to write a blessing prayer that can be done within the family. You might want to share with them some sample blessing prayers (verbally) and talk about themes/items to be included; you might not want to give them the prayers, as there might be a tendency to simply copy the prayer. Encourage their personal reflection and creativity.

After the prayers have been written, collect them, making copies and assembling them into a booklet of family blessings for each child/youth to take home with a bottle of holy water. Send home the handout as a way to encourage family blessings.

Prayer Together
God of all blessings, your Son, Jesus, welcomed and blessed the children. Continue to look with love on each of these children gathered here. May each one continue to grow in wisdom and grace, growing closer to you and united to everyone in your family. We ask this blessing, Loving God, through Jesus Christ, our Lord.

Option
Contact the parents before the book is assembled. Invite them to write a family blessing prayer to be included in the book.

Dear Parents,

Throughout our long Catholic history, holy water has often been taken home from church and kept there to be used in family blessings. The website of the U.S. bishops reminds us: "there are blessings that can be prayed by anyone who has been baptized, 'in virtue of the universal priesthood, a dignity they possess because of their baptism and confirmation' (Book of Blessings, no. 18). The blessings given by laypersons are exercised because of their special office, such as parents on behalf of their children."

After learning about the importance of water and the church's use of holy water, your children/youth have written some family blessing prayers that are contained in the booklet they are bringing home, along with a bottle of holy water. The prayers may be used in a number of ways:

- Trace the sign of the cross (with or without holy water) on the person's forehead
- Sprinkle holy water over the whole family
- Place your hands upon the head or shoulders of the person being blessed

We encourage you to keep the booklet and the holy water on your family meal table or with your family Bible for frequent use. You might also wish to purchase a holy water font to place near the door that your family uses most often throughout the day.

Thank you for the blessings that you are to each other in your family and to our parish community.

Gratefully in the extravagant blessings of our God,

Some Times and Reasons for Family Blessing Prayers

To begin a new day

Mealtimes

Bedtime

Before leaving the house

Birthdays

Baptismal anniversaries

Patron saint's day

To celebrate a special achievement

Time of illness

In times of trouble

The start of something new (new week, new school year, New Year's Day)

When grandparents visit

When friends visit

Blessing of home

New baby

A blessing for a car

Advent blessing

Valentine's Day

Ash Wednesday

Lenten blessing

Easter blessing

Mother's/Father's Day

On a great day

A blessing for strength

THE **WORKS** OF **MERCY**

Objective
To understand the Works of Mercy, discovering various ways to live them in daily life

Background for Catechists
Because we are the recipients of God's love and mercy, discipleship compels us to mirror God: to be loving and merciful to all in God's family.

The Corporal Works of Mercy are seven kind acts, helping our neighbors with their material and physical needs. The Spiritual Works of Mercy are seven acts of compassion, helping others with their emotional and spiritual needs.

The Works of Mercy flow from the teachings of Jesus and the practices of the church. They are derived from Jesus' teaching that "Blessed are the merciful, for they will receive mercy" (Mt 5:7), and the Great Commandment of love of God and love of neighbor (Mt 22:37–39).

The first six Corporal Works are rooted in the parable of the sheep and goats (Mt 25:31–46); the seventh was added as early as the third century based upon Tobit 1:16–17.

Materials
- ☐ Copies of handout
- ☐ Large sheets of paper
- ☐ Pencils, pens
- ☐ Crayons, markers

Lesson Starter
Say: *If someone loves and cares for you, what do you want to do in return? Perhaps this is one of the most important things about our faith: because we have been loved and cared for by God, we want—we are called—to act the same way toward others. Since earliest times, the church has reminded us of ways to show love: the Corporal and Spiritual Works of Mercy. Think about some of the ways you live the Works of Mercy in your everyday life:*

- *Sharing snacks and treats rather than keeping everything for yourself*
- *Donating clothes to the poor*
- *Taking meals to those who are sick*
- *Caring for your family and relatives when they are sick*
- *Helping people who are angry or sad or confused rather than judging or ignoring them*
- *Praying for your family and friends*

Living these works happens often with those we are closest to; following Jesus calls us to always go deeper. How can we practice these loving acts for more and more people, even those whom we do not know?

Activity
Divide the children into seven groups. Give each group one of the Corporal Works of Mercy (on another day you can do the same activity with the Spiritual Works). Invite each group to make an edition of a newspaper based solely on their Corporal Work: news stories (local, national, international), editorials, want ads, cartoon format, puzzles, letters to the editor, announcements, weather reports, entertainment section, etc.

Prayer Together
Lord, make me an instrument of your peace. Where there is hatred, let me sow your love. Where there is injury, pardon. Where there is doubt, faith. Where there is despair, hope. Where there is darkness, light. Where there is sadness, joy.

Options
- Display the newspapers at the parish or at local businesses.
- Instead of a newspaper, make a video or PowerPoint about the Work of Mercy.

The Corporal Works of Mercy

FEED THE HUNGRY

- Participate in a food drive
- Buy your favorite foods to give to a soup kitchen
- Bake cookies for a homeless shelter

GIVE DRINK TO THE THIRSTY

- Watch for ways to save water or keep it clean
- Hand out water at a race that raises money for a charity
- Help someone who is "thirsting" for a friend or someone to talk to

CLOTHE THE NAKED

- Participate in a coat collection
- Buy socks and underwear for people in homeless shelters
- Look for clothes on sale or non-name brands. Donate the money saved to an organization that helps people in need

SHELTER THE HOMELESS

- Participate in a Blanket Drive
- Participate in a Walk for the Homeless
- Send cards or gifts to new neighbors or parishioners

VISIT THE SICK

- Visit a nursing home
- Send a card to someone who is sick
- Prepare meals for Ronald McDonald House

VISIT THE IMPRISONED

- Collect books for a prison library
- Help someone who is "imprisoned" by a disability or handicap

BURY THE DEAD

- Call the local cemetery, asking if they need help with cleanup around the grounds
- See if there are any other ways to assist: putting flags out around Memorial Day or Veterans Day

The Spiritual Works of Mercy

ADMONISH THE SINNER

- Be a witness; refuse to take part in things you know are wrong
- Gently help others make good decisions

INSTRUCT THE IGNORANT

- Help a sibling with homework
- Share a gift/talent with another

COUNSEL THE DOUBTFUL

- Encourage someone who is down
- Share positive thoughts

COMFORT THE SORROWFUL

- Make a card for someone who is grieving
- Give comfort to those with sick loved ones
- Make a butterfly for someone who has died and give it to their relatives.

BEAR WRONGS PATIENTLY

- Turn the other cheek
- Don't get upset if you're treated unfairly

FORGIVE ALL INJURIES

- Reconcile with someone who has hurt you

PRAY FOR THE LIVING AND THE DEAD

- Make a prayer list, using it daily
- Pray for people listed in the church bulletin

OTHER TITLES IN THIS SERIES

Enriching Faith

Lessons and Activities on the Bible

Mary Kathleen Glavich, SND

Here are creative ways to introduce biblical lands and cultures, versions of the Bible, biblical reference tools, and techniques for using Scripture as a basis for prayer. Essential topical background, additional teaching ideas, and fun reproducible activity sheets make this a must-have resource, perfect for helping students in grades four and up develop a lifelong understanding and love for sacred Scripture.

72 PAGES | $14.95 | 9781627850278

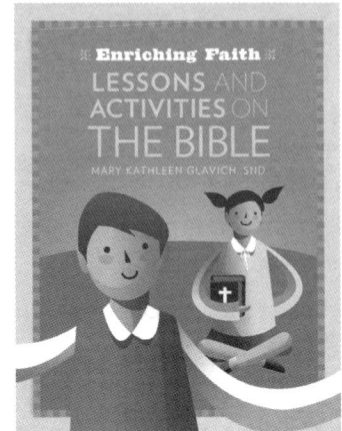

Enriching Faith

Lessons and Activities on Prayer

Catherine Stewart

Here are dozens of fresh ideas to help your students see prayer in a whole new light. Easy-to-do activities like the bouncing Prayer Ball, Gratitude Grab Bags, and Spoons of Thankfulness can help you teach traditional, spontaneous, creative, and even meditative prayer. Complete with directions, templates, discussion starters, parent letters, catechetical information, and much more.

72 PAGES | $14.95 | 9781585959471

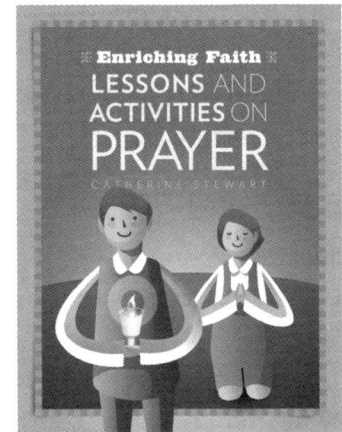

Enriching Faith

Prayers and Activities on Service

Patricia Mathson

Help children make Christian service a way of life with this creative collection of outreach projects, hands-on learning experiences, and joyful prayers. Each activity speaks to children's hearts and includes easy instructions, curriculum connections, and more. Perfect for parish, school, or home-based programs, and anyone who wants to help children become caring and compassionate followers of Christ.

72 PAGES | $14.95 | 9781585959372

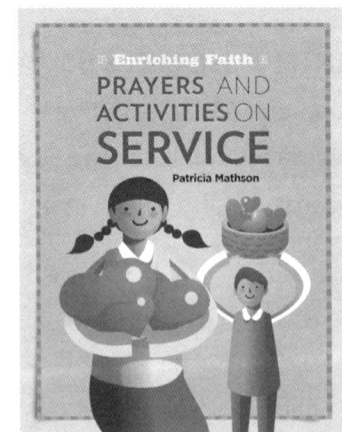

1-800-321-0411

23RDPUBLICATIONS.COM

TWENTY THIRD PUBLICATIONS